THE
HIDDEN
SUN

Para Ignacio,

Buena Suerte!

—James

THE HIDDEN SUN:

SOLAR ECLIPSES AND ASTRO- PHOTO- GRAPHY

JAMES LOWENTHAL

AVON
PUBLISHERS OF BARD, CAMELOT, DISCUS AND FLARE BOOKS

THE HIDDEN SUN is an original publication of Avon
Books. This work has never before appeared in book form.

AVON BOOKS
A division of
The Hearst Corporation
1790 Broadway
New York, New York 10019

First Avon Printing, June, 1984

AVON TRADEMARK REG. U.S. PAT. OFF. AND IN
OTHER COUNTRIES, MARCA REGISTRADA, HECHO EN
U.S.A.

Printed in the U.S.A.

DON 10 9 8 7 6 5 4 3 2 1

ACKNOWLEDGMENTS

Thanks first to Walter Meade for the idea. I appreciate Barry Gordon's many helpful suggestions. Thanks to Allen Seltzer for early guidance, Jack Vansickle for the telescope mount, and Sam Lipman for the refractor. I also appreciate the support and assistance of my editors, Liz Burpee, Jean Feiwel, Ellen Miles, and Kathryn Vought. I thank Wendy Kohn for her patience and suggestions. Finally, I thank my family for continuing support, even though I told them that their help was not the kind that gets mentioned in acknowledgments.

TABLE OF CONTENTS

PREFACE   11

Chapter 1. THE HIDDEN SUN—BLACKOUT '79   13
What is a solar eclipse? . . .
Photographing a solar eclipse

Chapter 2. EXPLORING THE STARS   37
Star trails . . . Clock-driven star photographs . . .
Star clusters . . . Summary

Chapter 3. LUNAR PHOTOGRAPHY   53
Prime focus . . . Projection systems . . .
Lunar eclipses . . . Summary and exposure chart

**Chapter 4. SOLAR PHOTOGRAPHY—The   65
UNeclipsed Sun**
Filters . . . Sunspots . . . Exposure calculations . . .
Summary

Chapter 5. PLANETARY PHOTOGRAPHY   71
What to look for . . . Summary and exposure chart

Chapter 6. REACHING DEEP INTO SPACE   77
Nebulae and galaxies . . . Summary

Chapter 7. ECLIPSE '80—INDIA   81
Experiencing eclipses . . . Before and after

APPENDIX I: Some Basic Terms   89
Angular size . . . Focal length . . . Focal ratio . . .
Celestial coordinates

APPENDIX II: Glossary   97

APPENDIX III: A Word on Films   103

APPENDIX IV: Some Other Reading   105

THE
HIDDEN
SUN

PREFACE

Most people have never heard the word *astrophotography*. Practically everybody has heard of *astronomy* and *photography*, though; so why not astrophotography? From a historical point of view, we have astrophotographs to thank for countless astronomical discoveries, such as the planet Pluto, hundreds of comets and asteroids, the detailed structure of distant galaxies and nebulae, and various other fascinating things in the far reaches of the universe. Although today most professional astronomical research is done by means other than photography—for example, X-ray and radio astronomy—photographs made by amateurs continue to produce data on all kinds of subjects like comets, the aurora borealis, meteors, and eclipses.

But leaving all this aside, there are other reasons to turn your camera to the heavens. When you go on a trip during a vacation, you might see a beautiful landscape and wish to take a correspondingly beautiful picture of it. Or maybe you just want pictures to remind you of your trip. The same with astrophotography. It is simply very gratifying to get back a roll of film from the processor and to find that you have finally captured a gorgeous image of the Moon, Sun, or Jupiter, or of a particular constellation. Astronomical photographs are very often stunningly beautiful pictures, as you can see by leafing through this book. What is more, astrophotos are not always difficult to take. Although some celestial camera subjects require fairly sophisticated equipment, there are also some that can be photographed with the bare minimum of camera and tripod.

The reason I begin this book with solar eclipses, a subject that is not entirely simple, is that eclipses are particularly favorite subjects for me, and so I hope will serve as an appealing introduction to astrophotography. In fact, I am an "eclipse

11

junkie," one of those crazy astronomers who will travel all over
the world to watch the Moon pass in front of the Sun for a few
minutes. I can think of no other natural event that is more
thrilling and awesome.

In this book, I provide information to enable a nonas-
tronomer to take successful astrophotographs. This is not an
astronomy textbook, however, nor does it teach the reader
everything about telescopes. Nor does it offer a complete gal-
lery of astrophotography. I like to think of writing this book as
sharing with you my personal journal of sky photography over
the past several years. It doesn't span the entire spectrum of
current amateur astrophotography, but it does provide a sound
base.

People with a wide range of photographic and astronomical
experience and equipment can take astronomical photographs.
For some subjects, a 35-mm rangefinder camera, a locking
cable release, and a tripod will be enough, while for others ac-
cess to a telescope and a camera with reflex focusing (such as a
35-mm single-lens reflex) is necessary. In most cases, some fa-
miliarity with photography is useful but not necessary. In all
cases, I wish you the best of luck and eternally clear skies.

JAMES LOWENTHAL
Bridgewater, CT
December, 1983

CHAPTER 1

· ·

THE HIDDEN SUN—
BLACKOUT '79

My roommate and I awoke at 5 A.M., half an hour before the wake-up call from the Yogo Inn desk. We had both slept fitfully, as we had for the past two nights; anxiety prevented deep sleep. We peered out the window hopefully and shouted with relief to see Venus flash brilliantly through crystal-clear skies. The clouds of the past three days had vanished. To us, good weather meant one thing: a chance to see the total solar eclipse of February 26, 1979.

After forcing some breakfast into our jumpy stomachs, we met with the rest of our group in the hotel lobby, loaded our considerable numbers of tripods, telescopes, and cameras onto the two charter busses, and boarded at 6:30 A.M. Despite the clarity of the skies earlier in the morning, some high clouds moving in from the west confirmed the weather reports, and we decided to move east at the last minute—we were going to chase the eclipse! After a nerve-wracking half hour of waiting in the busses, our group of more than seventy-five drove out of Lewistown, Montana, followed by six or seven carloads of fellow eclipse chasers, who were also looking for a better observing site.

We, the Amateur Observers' Society (A.O.S.) of New York City, had been the talk of Lewistown for nearly a year—we and the eclipse, of course. It had all started when an official from the A.O.S. had notified the town fathers that Lewistown appeared to be an ideal place for viewing the upcoming celestial event. In the first place, Lewistown was situated precisely on the center line of the path of totality, the narrow band along which one must be stationed to see the Sun entirely eclipsed by the Moon. There, the eclipse would last for almost the maximum observable time. Secondly, the weather prospects, according to data compiled over several years, were that the chance of clear skies at that location was well above fifty-fifty for that time of year—certainly far better than the cloud cover predicted for Washington, Oregon, and other states over which the eclipse would pass. Although the areas of Canada where the eclipse would be visible shared equal or better weather forecasts, the thought of bitter cold, far worse even than the notorious Montana winter for which we were prepared, convinced many of us that the Lewistown area was the place to be. As it happened, we arrived in Great Falls, Montana, on the 23rd of February to be greeted with the news that Lewistown itself had had the distinction of the nation's lowest temperature for that day: twenty-eight degrees below zero, centigrade (−18 degrees Fahrenheit).

After learning of its favorable location, the city of 6,500 got right on the ball. Soon the slogan "Lewistown—Eclipse Capital of the World" was adopted and widely publicized. Before long, many had seized and capitalized on the idea: eclipse peanut brittle, eclipse patches and T-shirts, and eclipse discount sales were to be found throughout Lewistown. Eclipse seminars, sleigh rides, and torchlight parades were planned, the small police force was enlarged, and businesses and hotels geared up for the tremendous crowds that were expected to come to see the spectacle.

And people did travel from the world over to see this eclipse, as they do to regions far more remote than Lewistown, Montana. There were several from overseas, and one man had even hitchhiked all the way from Boston.

People often ask, "You went way out there *just to see an eclipse?*"

"But of course," we answer. "A total eclipse of the Sun is perhaps the most awesome of all Nature's spectacles," we try to explain.

There were quite a few reasons for this particular event's popularity, especially among Americans. In the first place, it was in the nation's own backyard. The path of totality passed through the states of Washington, Oregon, Idaho, Montana, and North Dakota, as well as through the middle of Canada.

In the second place, this would be the last total eclipse of the Sun visible in North America until the year 2017. Many people realized this was their last chance for a long time to see a total solar eclipse without traveling long distances.

Many who came to the Lewistown area traveled on their own, while others were part of groups organized especially to see the eclipse. The advantages of traveling with a full-fledged expedition are many. If well conducted, of course, the expedition will have made all hotel and airline reservations, chartered busses, and so on, saving individuals the trouble of taking care of such necessities.

Of greater importance, usually, are the specific attractions a particular expedition may offer. These may include not only special seminars, lectures, or the presence of famous scholars and professors, but also "chase" vehicles and, sometimes, meteorologists. The chances of seeing the eclipse are greatly enhanced if you have mobility in case of inclement weather. Bad weather is the most hated enemy of the eclipse chaser, but many an eclipse that would otherwise have been clouded out has been seen thanks to the availability of quick emergency transportation to a place of clear skies. This is an obvious advantage of the cruise ships that can carry passengers to the center line of totality in the middle of an ocean. If the weather prospects aren't good, the ship, often aided by satellite weather information, merely travels along the path of totality until a break in the clouds is found.

The rising sun of February 26, 1979, was greeted with much applause from the passengers of the A.O.S. chase busses. After riding for an hour along narrow roads with snow piled high on either side, we arrived in the small town of Roy, Montana, with a minimum of time in which to set up. First contact was to occur at 8:21 A.M. We obtained permission from a farmer to set up our equipment in his hay field, and soon we had poured out of the busses, invaded the field, and hurriedly planted our tripods, telescopes, cameras, and multitudes of other equipment in the crusty snow.

At last someone started a countdown: ". . . three, two, one—first contact!" The eclipse had begun!

At first, no change was visible. Within ten or fifteen seconds, though, a small indentation appeared on the Sun's disk at about the two-o'clock position; the edge of the Moon's disk had begun to encroach on the Sun. Shutters clicked and people chattered nervously—there was light cloud cover over the entire sky, and eclipses have been known to be blocked out by the only cloud on an otherwise clear day. As the Moon devoured more and more of the Sun, however, the clouds seemed to dissipate as if in honor of the grand celestial spectacle that was taking place.

The next hour flew by. Now, the familiar round Sun had been reduced to a brilliant crescent, still thousands of times too bright to view with the unprotected eye. We watched the progress of the eclipse through exposed and developed film and pieces of aluminized Mylar (see the section in Chapter 4 on photographing the sun). The sky had turned an eerie metallic green-gray, and the earth, too, took on a thin, unnatural color.

Five minutes before totality, the light was dramatically reduced and the temperature dropped several degrees to 2 degrees centigrade (35 degrees Fahrenheit). A sudden cry of "There's the shadow!" turned all heads to the southeast. Sure enough, the mountains on the horizon had been plunged into darkness. There was the sharply defined shadow of the Moon, rushing toward us at an incredible 2,400 kilometers per hour—25 miles per minute! A second countdown was called out, but the razor-thin crescent of Sun still blazed forth. The countdown had been off by a whole minute—we had forgotten to account for our travel eastward.

Totality was now only seconds away. All filters were off, all eyes turned up. Then, as we watched, the intense flare of sunlight grew smaller and smaller and was suddenly extinguished like a magnificent candle. At the same time, the awesome shadow of the Moon rushed over our heads, a cloak of night-time, a funnel of darkness. This was the moment, we had been told, when experienced eclipse chasers, even the calmest of them, snap their camera shutters without winding the film, knock down their tripods in excitement, or forget entirely about their carefully prepared equipment.

As we were overwhelmed by the Moon's shadow, the halo of luminous gas surrounding the Sun appeared magically in sharp relief against the dull sky, a pearly white corona. Its ghostly streamers radiated outward, and intricate loops and swirls were visible in spite of the haze. Even more impressive than the corona were the prominences, crimson tongues of flame licking out from the Sun and rimming the edge of the sil-houetted Moon. They were larger and more plentiful than any of us had expected. The sight of those spectacular fires drew shouts and cries from the exuberant crowd below. As the Moon moved across the face of the Sun, the deep red prominences seemed to writhe.

Ever since second contact I had been clicking away at the camera I had attached to my 5-cm refracting telescope. Well be-fore departing for Montana, I had practiced my picture-taking pattern for the brief moments of totality: I was to start with a certain shutter speed, then take longer and longer exposures until the end of totality, so that I could record both the bright-est and the faintest of phenomena. I had calculated that I would have just enough time to take sixteen shots between second contact and third contact—the beginning and the ending of to-tality—and now I was alternately pressing the cable release, looking through the camera/telescope eyepiece for a close-up view of the prominences, and letting out ear-splitting whoops of delight and excitement.

For those who could bear to tear their eyes away from the enthralling Sun, the bright stars of the Summer Triangle were winking faintly in the February sky and Venus shone for the second time that day. Overhead, the sky was a deep blue-black, like a bright moonlit night, but the horizons were untouched by the shadow: There seemed to be a 360-degree sunset, with weird copper and magenta colors encircling the land in the shadow. Usually the relatively faint light from the chromosphere, the deep red portion of the Sun surrounding the central photosphere, is overpowered by the photosphere's light. During second and third contacts of a total solar eclipse, however, the photosphere is hidden by the Moon, allowing the chromosphere to be seen for a few seconds. The parts of the horizon that we saw to be doused in coppery "sunset" colors were actually illuminated by the chromosphere.

Perhaps most memorable of all, however, was the sight of the eclipsed Sun itself. To see such a strange, beautiful object in the middle of a clear, daytime, and yet dark sky is not an experience to be forgotten soon.

As third contact, the end of totality, approached, the right-hand edge of the Sun showed more and more, revealing the scarlet chromosphere. And then, suddenly, a burst of sunlight exploded around the edge of the Moon, forming the stunning diamond-ring effect. The corona seemed to collapse, the prominences were overwhelmed by the dazzle, and then thin daylight returned rapidly. The solar crescent quickly gained size as the Moon withdrew across the Sun's face. Triumphant cheers filled the air. Some people even cried for sheer joy.

During the course of the next hour or so, the crescent Sun grew and grew until finally the last sliver of light had been restored. But people had already packed up much of their equipment, and we had our last looks at the now-sun-bathed field and boarded the busses. As we headed back to Lewistown, exhausted, we thought of the huge secret we had just shared, and some of us made plans for the next eclipse expedition to Africa and India the following February.

People say that once you have seen a total eclipse of the Sun you have been "bitten by the bug" and are compelled to see more. Indeed, the next day, as I boarded the plane to Newark, New Jersey, from Great Falls, I shook hands with a certain veteran eclipse chaser. This had been his eighth eclipse. "See you in Kenya," he said with a grin.

What is a solar eclipse? A solar eclipse occurs when the Moon, traveling in its orbit around Earth, passes in front of the Sun and blocks out part or all of the bright part we normally see, the photosphere (see Figure 1). By true heavenly coincidence, the disk of the Moon seems to us virtually the same diameter as that of the Sun; although the Sun is 400 times larger than the Moon, the Moon is 400 times closer to Earth. This means that, when the lunar disk is perfectly superimposed on the solar disk, parts of the Sun normally too dim to be seen next to the glare of the brilliant photosphere become visible during the brief period of totality, when the photosphere is completely covered.

In order to see the total phase of an eclipse, you must be stationed somewhere in the path of the umbra, the darkest part of the Moon's shadow. The widest possible diameter of the umbra at Earth's surface is 269 km, although, if the shadow strikes the surface obliquely, it is projected as an ellipse and so can be longer than it is wide. As the Moon moves around Earth in its orbit, the shadow describes a narrow band across Earth's surface—that is the path of totality. Near the center of the path, totality lasts the longest, while at the precise edge of the path there will be merely an instant of totality. Totality can never last much more than seven minutes and is usually much shorter.

Often the umbra just misses the Earth but the penumbra, the lighter part of the shadow, does sweep across portions of the globe. This results in a partial solar eclipse: Observers standing in the penumbra can see part, but not all, of the Sun. The closer one gets to the umbra, the less of the Sun one can see.

In some cases, the Moon is centered precisely in front of the Sun but is too far away from the observer to cover it completely. In other words, the umbra isn't long enough at the time of eclipse to touch the Earth's surface. During these eclipses one sees a narrow, bright ring of photosphere surrounding the black disk of the Moon; this is called an annular eclipse. Although they are actually more frequent than total eclipses, annular eclipses are usually less interesting because the photosphere is not completely hidden. No corona, chromosphere, prominences, or diamond rings are seen, and filters must still be used.

The orbits of and distances between Earth, Moon, and Sun are so well known that scientists can predict the type, duration,

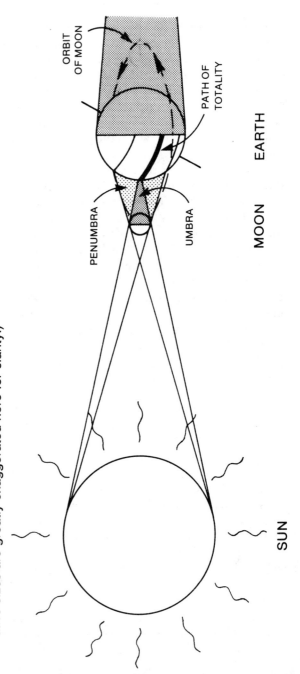

Figure 1. A TOTAL SOLAR ECLIPSE occurs when the Moon passes between Earth and the Sun. The Sun is totally blocked from the view of an observer stationed anywhere in the umbra; an observer in the penumbra can see part of the Sun. As the Moon orbits the Earth, the umbra traces the path of totality shown. (Relative sizes are greatly exaggerated here for clarity.)

and precise paths of eclipses literally centuries in advance. Because of the restrictions of the orbits, there can be at most seven eclipses in one year, of which either four or five are of the Sun, the rest being of the Moon (see Chapter 3). There must be at least two eclipses of the Sun each year, but, because the path of totality is so narrow, a total solar eclipse can be seen only once every 360 years (on the average) from any one particular place on the Earth.

"So what?" you ask. "What's the point of traveling thousands of miles just to see the Sun get lost for a couple of minutes?"

That's not the point. It's what you *can* see, not what you *can't,* that is the excitement of the total solar eclipse. Let's take a look at what you can see, and why.

The Sun is composed of several layers differing in heat, depth, composition, and color. The highly luminous, white surface of the Sun, the sharp disk that one sees through a dark filter, is called the *photosphere.* It is the photosphere that emits most of the Sun's visible light. Composed mostly of hydrogen, helium, and some other elements, its outer limits are almost 700,000 km in radius, or 108 times Earth's radius. The temperature there is 5,800 degrees Kelvin—5,527 degrees centigrade or about 10,000 degrees Fahrenheit.

Surrounding the photosphere is the *chromosphere,* extending above the former about 2,000 km. Although the chromosphere is generally much hotter than the photosphere, varying between 4,500 K and 10,000 K, it is much dimmer. Its characteristic deep red color, emitted by hydrogen-alpha, is usually completely lost in the glare of the blinding photosphere.

Reaching out from the chromosphere are the *flares* and *prominences,* spectacular arcs and mountains of solar material erupting from the Sun's surface or falling back to it from the corona. They, too, are the deep red of hydrogen-alpha. Some have been known to reach heights of 300,000 km, more than twenty-five times Earth's diameter.

At its outer reaches, the chromosphere begins to blend with the *corona,* the outer atmosphere of the Sun extending beyond the photosphere for millions of kilometers and merging gradu-

Table 1 SOLAR ECLIPSES FROM 1984 TO 2000

Date	Type of eclipse[1]	Magnitude (if partial)[2]	Maximum duration of totality (if any) min.	sec.	Path of totality or annularity[3]
1984 May 30	annular	—	—	—	Pacific Ocean, No. America, NW Africa
1984 Nov. 22	total	—	1	59	Indonesia, So. Pacific Ocean
1985 May 19	partial	0.841	—	—	—
1985 Nov. 12	total	—	1	59	So. Pacific Ocean
1986 April 09	partial	0.823	—	—	—
1986 Oct. 03	annular	—	—	—	No. Atlantic Ocean
1987 March 29	annular	—	—	—	So. America, Atlantic Ocean, Africa
1987 Sept. 23	annular	—	—	—	Asia, China, Pacific Ocean
1988 March 18	total	—	3	46	Indian Ocean, Indonesia, No. Pacific
1988 Sept. 11	annular	—	—	—	Indian Ocean, Antarctic coast
1989 March 07	partial	0.827	—	—	—
1989 Aug. 31	partial	0.634	—	—	—
1990 Jan. 26	annular	—	—	—	Antarctica, So. Atlantic Ocean
1990 July 22	total	—	2	33	No. Europe, No. Asia, No. Pacific Ocean
1991 Jan. 15	annular	—	—	—	Australia, New Zealand, Pacific Ocean
1991 July 11	total	—	6	54	Pacific Ocean, Hawaii, Mexico, So. America
1992 Jan. 04	annular	—	—	—	Pacific Ocean
1992 June 30	total	—	5	20	So. Atlantic Ocean
1992 Dec. 24	partial	0.842	—	—	—

Year	Date	Type	Magnitude	Min.	Sec.	Region
1993	May 21	partial	0.736	—	—	—
1993	Nov. 13	partial	0.928	—	—	—
1994	May 10	annular	—	—	—	Pacific Ocean, No. America, Atlantic Ocean, NW Africa
1994	Nov. 03	total	—	—	—	Pacific Ocean, So. America, So. Atlantic Ocean
1995	April 29	annular	—	—	—	Pacific Ocean, So. America, Atlantic Ocean
1995	Oct. 24	total	—	2	10	Middle and Far East, India, Malaysia, Pacific Ocean
1996	April 17	partial	0.879	—	—	—
1996	Oct. 12	partial	0.757	—	—	—
1997	March 09	total	—	2	50	Siberia, Arctic Ocean
1997	Sept. 02	partial	0.899	—	—	—
1998	Feb. 26	total	—	4	08	Pacific Ocean, Caribbean Sea, Atlantic Ocean
1998	Aug. 22	annular	—	—	—	Indian Ocean, Indonesia, New Zealand, Pacific Ocean
1999	Feb. 16	annular	—	—	—	Indian Ocean, Australia
1999	Aug. 11	total	—	2	23	Atlantic Ocean, Europe, Middle East, India
2000	Feb. 05	partial	0.579	—	—	—
2000	July 01	partial	0.477	—	—	—
2000	July 31	partial	0.603	—	—	—
2000	Dec. 25	partial	0.723	—	—	—

[1]See pp. 18–19

[2]The *magnitude* of a partial eclipse is the maximum fraction of the Sun's disk that is eclipsed.

[3]Detailed information, including maps, of the paths of all these eclipses is compiled by the U.S. Naval Observatory. You can get it by writing to: United States Naval Observatory, Washington, D.C. 20390.

ally with the vacuum of space. It is a gaseous, incandescent envelope consisting of dozens of highly ionized elements. Despite its intense heat—about a million degrees K—its intensity in the visible-light spectrum is very low, about the same as that of the Full Moon; most of its radiation is high-energy, in the region of X rays. Thus, like the chromosphere, the corona is virtually invisible next to the brilliant photosphere.

During a total solar eclipse, the glaring light from the photosphere is precisely blocked by the Moon, allowing the dimmer chromosphere, the corona, the prominences, and the flares to be seen clearly. It is largely for the view of such rarely seen phenomena that eclipse chasers travel the world over.

By no means, however, are the attractions limited to the Sun itself. Indeed, one problem many people have is deciding what to look for in the few brief moments of totality. Let us run through the various stages of a typical solar eclipse.

First contact occurs when the leading edge, or limb, of the Moon first "touches" the edge of the Sun (see Figure 2). As time goes on, the Moon covers more and more of the Sun's face, gradually reducing it to a crescent that in turn grows thinner and thinner. Depending on the conditions of the weather and the particular eclipse, there will be a noticeable change in the quality and density of the daylight. It is debatable at what point there is a noticeable change in Earth's atmosphere; people who are prepared for an eclipse might be influenced by the power of suggestion in observing changes in the light around them. The light itself is usually a green-gray color. Many describe it as "electric," "eerie," "tense"—it usually is all these. Often, the surrounding landscape looks as if a summer electrical storm were about to break. All these phenomena become more pronounced as totality approaches.

Only ten minutes or so after first contact, if you cross your hands with the fingers slightly spread, so that you create many small holes, the shadow your hands cast upon the ground will show an image of the partially eclipsed Sun for each hole. This is because each opening in your hands is working like a pinhole camera or a small lens, each one forming an inverted image of the Sun. Trees and bushes also show this effect; scattered on the ground in the sun-dappled shadow will be dozens of identical images of the solar crescent. This effect becomes clearer and clearer as the crescent diminishes.

Great care must be taken to protect your eyes from the serious damage looking at the Sun can cause. Whenever there is photosphere showing, such as during the entire partial phase, high-intensity radiation is streaming forth, as explained in Chapter 4. To see the noneclipsed Sun or to watch the progress of the partial-eclipse phase, you must either project the solar image with a telescope as described below or, if you want to ob-

Figure 2.   THE SEQUENCE OF EVENTS during a total solar eclipse. The Moon's motion is not always from right to left, as shown here, but depends on the relationship of Earth, Moon, and Sun at the time of the eclipse. If the Moon's apparent diameter is smaller than the Sun's at the time of eclipse because the Moon's orbit has carried it farther away from Earth, an "annular" eclipse occurs. (The difference in apparent sizes is exaggerated here for clarity.)

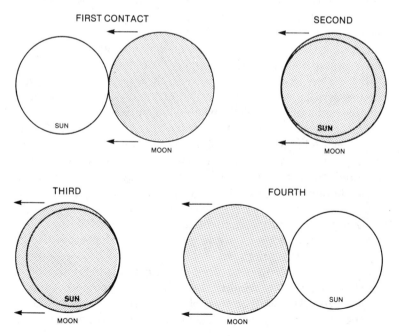

serve the Sun directly, look through a dense filter or position one in front of your telescope or your camera.

The first method, projection with a telescope, is certainly the safer way, although you won't see as much detail. To obtain an image, hold a piece of white cardboard a foot or so from the eyepiece of the telescope and then focus the image projected on the "screen" by adjusting the eyepiece. The crescent of the partial eclipse will be clearly seen. The image will be clearest if you shade the cardboard from direct sunlight.

For the second method, direct observation, you will need a very dense filter, probably one made expressly for the purpose. A few types are described in Chapter 4. Sometimes an eclipse expedition will supply them to its members. In Montana, one staff astronomer had very fully exposed and developed several dozen pieces of black-and-white sheet film, which he distributed to the crowd of eclipse chasers. This is a safe solar filter. Another popular solution is common welder's glass, providing it is dense enough; a density of 5 is usually about right. This corresponds to a welder's glass No. 12, No. 13, or No. 14.

Fortunately for the eclipse chaser, totality is strictly naked-eye time—no filter is required for the exciting part. In fact, you must make sure to remove filters from any equipment you may have brought along, such as cameras and telescopes, before totality comes, or else the dim corona, chromosphere, and prominences will be completely blacked out and you will miss your photographs or your close-up viewing entirely. You must remember to *replace the filters after totality,* of course. A generally accepted rule is that within one minute of totality it is all right to glance at the crescent briefly with the naked eye. Keep in mind, though, that the more you gaze at the brilliant crescent, the longer it will take for your eyes to adapt to the darkness of totality.

The partial phase usually lasts about an hour, give or take a few minutes. It is near the end of the partial phase that things really start happening fast.

The planets Venus and Mercury become visible in the darkened sky well before totality. In addition, you may see several bright stars. They will be stars of constellations you are used to seeing in an entirely different season, at which time of the year the Sun's brightness doesn't outshine them. It pays to find out beforehand which stars will be in the sky at the time of the eclipse, so that you will know what to look for.

As second contact—the point at which the Moon first covers the solar disk completely—approaches, things get even more exciting. If you watch the ground carefully, starting several minutes before totality, you might see the elusive and infrequent shadow bands. Those who have seen them describe them as vague, dark bands wavering or shimmering across the ground. Sometimes they are distinct bands, sometimes they have just a hint of movement, like rippling water. They are best seen on large, light-colored surfaces such as a patch of sand. If you are intent on seeing shadow bands, bring a white sheet to the eclipse, stretch it out facing the Sun, and keep your eye on it immediately before and after totality. Shadow bands are virtually impossible to photograph because of their low contrast and high speed. It would be more worth your while to turn your camera toward other aspects of the eclipse.

About a minute or so before totality, the Moon's shadow itself may first become visible. You will see a tremendous area of darkness rushing toward you. It will blacken everything it touches, and its closest edge will seem to take a direct bearing on the remaining sliver of solar crescent. Sometimes the shadow is not visible at all; often its conical shape is clearly defined. It seems to depend on atmospheric conditions, and it is difficult to predict whether or not the shadow will be easy to see.

A few seconds before second contact, mountain peaks and other high spots of the Moon's edge make the thin solar crescent seem to break apart just before the entire crescent disappears. The effect is that of a brilliant, shimmering, string of beads, and has been named for Francis Baily (1774–1844), who observed and described it. *Baily's Beads* can sometimes be seen for several seconds, sometimes not at all; their presence or absence depends on the profile of the Moon at the time of the eclipse.

Then, at the same time the shadow rushes over you the last flash of brilliant photosphere will shine through a valley or between two mountains of the Moon. At that time the inner corona, the brightest part of the Sun's gaseous envelope, will fade into view around the Moon's disk. The coronal ring and the single flash of photosphere bear a striking resemblance to a sparkling *diamond ring*. The beautiful diamond-ring stage may last as long as several seconds or may fade away almost immediately, depending, like Baily's Beads, on the silhouette of the Moon's disk.

As the last flash of photosphere fades from view, totality has officially arrived. Now the full corona itself appears around the black, black disk of the Moon.

The size and shape of the corona depend on the stage the Sun is in at the time. The Sun has cycles of magnetic activity that take about eleven years from maximum to maximum. At minimum, there are few sunspots (and so, few solar prominences) and the corona is relatively small. In addition, the corona is likely to be asymmetrical: There will be longer wisps of coronal material reaching away from the Sun at its equator, while from its magnetic poles there will be shorter, but probably more clearly defined, streamers. At maximum, the corona is likely to be both larger and more symmetrical.

The corona is brightest closest to the Sun's face. As your eyes become dark-adapted after having been exposed to the relatively bright light of the partial phase, you will be able to see more and more of the fainter regions until by the end of totality the corona will seem larger to you than it did at the beginning. Details to look for include the streamers, transients (or loops in the coronal material), and other intricacies that may be different from one eclipse to another.

For the most part, the corona is pure white or pearly white, although the color you observe can take on different shades as a result of atmospheric conditions. Many color photographs lend the corona a blueish tint, especially around the edges. This is usually a fault of the film.

Another major attraction of total solar eclipses is the deep red of the prominences. Most prominences are associated with particular sunspot groups; so more prominences can be seen at a period of maximum solar activity than at a period of minimum activity. The only way to see them, other than traveling to the center line of a total eclipse, is to view the Sun through a costly narrow-band-pass filter that transmits only a very specific wavelength of light. In this case it is the wavelength emitted by hydrogen-alpha, the stuff of solar prominences. The travel-to-the-center line method, however, requires merely the attention of your naked eye to see the magnificent prominences clearly.

Another aspect of total eclipses that varies from one to another is the amount of light cast on the observer and his surroundings during totality. Sometimes the landscape is as bright as if illuminated by a Full Moon, or even brighter, while sometimes it is too dark to read. Fortunately, you probably won't be doing a great deal of reading during totality. The darkness might pose a problem, though, if you had to see such things as the numbers on the shutter-speed dial of your camera or any exposure guide you might have written up for yourself. To this end, it is a good idea to be prepared with a small flashlight equipped with a red light bulb (the bulb can be painted with nail polish or covered with a piece of red cellophane); the red light won't ruin the night sight you acquire as totality progresses, but it will provide enough light for you to see your equipment if the eclipse happens to be particularly dark.

Once the total phase of the eclipse has passed the halfway time, the events occur in reverse. Gradually, prominences are revealed on the other limb of the Sun—the edge that will soon appear around the Moon. This section grows brighter all too soon; one senses that the Sun will shortly burst out at that particular point. The chromosphere will again be visible for a few moments. If you can bear to tear your eyes from the Sun you will see the trailing edge of the Moon's conical shadow drawing nearer and the horizon behind it returned to full daylight.

Then, sadly, the quickly dimming corona will be pierced by the first brilliant needles of sunlight, perhaps showing another display of Baily's Beads. The corona will shrink rapidly in the glare of the pure, clear, white photosphere, perhaps forming a diamond-ring effect with a bright blaze of sunlight. Then the solar crescent—stunningly white and razor sharp—will broaden quickly, flooding the view with thin daylight. Now is the time to put your filters back in front of your eyes and your equipment. Shadow bands may appear again. You will be a good deal more sensitive to the phenomena of third contact, since there will have been several minutes for your eyes to dark-adapt.

After third contact the partial phase proceeds in reverse, with the Sun being restored to its normal round self in a matter of an hour or so. Although hardly an everyday occurrence, this part of the eclipse is anticlimactic to the earlier phases and draws relatively little attention from most eclipse chasers. Many will swear they'll stay until the last chink of Sun has been restored, but, come the last partial phase, most tend to pack up equipment and call it a day.

Why and how do you photograph a solar eclipse? There are many reasons why you might wish to do it. In the first place, all your friends will be eager to see proof that you really traipsed to Siberia, Montana, the South Pole, or wherever, and that your efforts weren't fruitless (assuming they weren't).

Also, it's usually quite exciting to see one's own photos of the magnificent event; there's nothing like a slide show of the eclipse to transport you back to the expedition, to the very observing site itself.

Finally, a photograph tends to hold a great deal of information that you may well have missed in the excitement of totality. In the privacy of your own home you will be able to study the prominences and the coronal streamers at length. You may see details that escaped notice entirely during the eclipse itself. During the Montana eclipse, for example, there was a coronal transient at about the two-o'clock position. This magnetic "bubble" had never before been photographed because the last time one occurred had been over a century ago, before the advent of eclipse photography. The transient had not been noticed during the Blackout '79 expedition, but a professional astronomer who saw our slides pointed it out, appearing as a loop in the corona, in photographs by every one of us.

As to the how? Just about any camera and lens will give you some kind of satisfactory eclipse photo—provided you do your part well enough as photographer. So varied are the events during a total eclipse that there is a suitable target for the simplest instant-load family camera or the most elaborate telescope-camera combination. You can choose your target to suit your equipment, or you can let the desired subject dictate what equipment you will need, if you can afford it. Whatever the camera, though, you will want a tripod or some other camera support.

It almost goes without saying that eclipse film is color film. There is breathtaking color in all aspects of totality—corona, chromosphere, prominences, and so on—so be prepared with a film that offers good color rendition and resolution. Slow, fine-grain "slide" films (films that give transparent positive images) are excellent, although you may want something faster if you have a very high f/ratio system (more about this later) or want to capture lots of faint detail. It is important in any case to be prepared with a two-hour game plan. You should have enough film, and you should arrange your sequence so as not to finish a roll in the middle of totality.

To photograph the partial phases, you will need to reduce the intensity of the sunlight by a factor of at least several thousand. This involves the same methods as does photography of the everyday, uneclipsed Sun described in Chapter 4. Even though the crescent becomes thinner and thinner as the eclipse progresses, any part of the solar crescent is just as bright as if it were not eclipsed at all. (The very last part of the crescent to be devoured by the Moon will appear darker than the rest, however, because it is part of the solar limb and obeys the phenomenon of limb-darkening, which is also explained in Chapter 4.)

Since you will be using dense filters for the partial phases, it will be hard to include any kind of landscape in the same picture with the crescent Sun. You could try some elaborate double exposures, but probably you will find it best to stick with just the Sun alone. This will lead you to look for something more than a normal focal length in camera lenses. The tiny spot a "normal" (or "standard") lens makes of the Sun would be virtually lost in the expanse of the rest of the picture. A reasonable minimum focal length needed to capture any detail on the solar surface, or of the phenomena during totality, is 300 mm. (Formulas for figuring image size are given in Appendix I under *Focal length*.)

Probably you will want to plan a strategy that will capture

the progress of the partial stage through a series of shots taken at regular intervals. In each shot, the solar crescent will be thinner than in the preceding one until the last picture before totality, which will show the narrowest sliver of all.

It is a good idea to make a few test exposures of the noneclipsed Sun well in advance of the eclipse, using the same lens-filter-film combination you plan to use for the partial phase. This way, you will know exactly which exposure is right for your own equipment and save yourself the time- and film-consuming procedure of bracketing, or taking several exposures of different durations.

If you don't have a 300-mm telephoto lens, though, there is no reason to throw away your small camera in despair. One rather effective method of recording a total solar eclipse *requires* the use of its opposite—a wide-angle lens. In this technique, a single multiple exposure shows, in a dozen or so images in the same frame, the eclipse from beginning to end, with one image of the total phase in the middle of the picture. A filter is used in all the exposures of the partial phases, but it must be removed for the shot of totality; otherwise, the relatively dim corona would be entirely filtered out. To use this method, be sure your camera can handle multiple exposures. Also, you should become familiar with the techniques involved in making a shot like this because you want to be sure to get a smooth line of solar images across the photograph. (Many cameras have ways to cock the shutter without advancing the film; but sometimes the film does get moved, and the row of crescents weaves drunkenly across the frame.)

If you don't want to squeeze the entire eclipse into one multiple-exposure photograph and do want to capture more solar detail, you might use a lens of longer focal length—perhaps 100 mm or so. This will mean that the progress of the eclipse, as Sun and Moon travel through their two hours or so of motion across the sky, will not fit from beginning to end in one shot because of the narrower field of view of a longer focal length. In general, the Sun moves through about 30 degrees of arc (see *Angular size* in Appendix I) during those two hours. You will have to start the multiple-exposure photograph with the Sun already well into the crescent phase and end well before fourth contact, the very end of the last partial phase (look again at Figure 2).

You might want to capture the landscape on film as second contact approaches, bringing the Moon's shadow with it. If you want to photograph the shadow itself, you will do well to have as wide-angled a lens as possible. As for most other parts of an eclipse experience, a series of images presents the best method of showing the shadow's arrival: In each shot, the diagonal line of the shadow's leading edge will have eaten up more of the scene.

Another effective use of a short-focal-length lens providing a wide angle of view is for shots of totality itself. With the eclipsed Sun at the top of the field of view, the strange colors of the sky and the landscape can produce quite a scene. With the camera mounted on a sturdy tripod—as always in eclipse photography—start your series several seconds before second contact, so that you will capture the shadow (if visible), the diamond ring, and all the phenomena of totality. While you can choose your exposures from the graph in Table 2 according to your specific targets, there is a more popular and almost invariably successful method, as follows:

Starting with a high shutter speed at the beginning of totality, work your way down through the whole range of speeds your camera is capable of, so that in the middle of totality you will be using the lowest shutter speed you have. Then work your way back up through the whole range of speeds, thus being prepared for third contact with an appropriately high shutter speed. This way, you will have at least one shot for every shutter speed you have. Since the aspects of totality vary tremendously in brightness, a different shutter speed is needed for each one. By using this exaggerated form of bracketing, you are assured of getting an exposure for virtually every aspect of the eclipse. The relatively high shutter speed with which you begin and end your series can either be the highest your camera has, or you can choose it from Table 2 to expose for the diamond ring or the prominences. If the eclipse is going to be a rather short one, or if you merely want to watch more and click shutters less, you might want to halve the number of exposures by skipping every other shutter-speed setting. In short, you can tailor your method to suit your needs.

Table 2

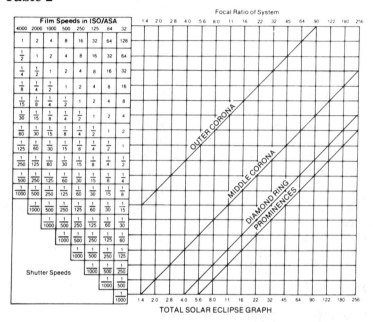

Film Speeds in ISO/ASA — Shutter Speeds — Focal Ratio of System

TOTAL SOLAR ECLIPSE GRAPH

To get real detail of the eclipsed Sun itself, you really need a long lens of some sort. Whether this be a telephoto lens bought to fit your camera or a telescope with camera body attached by one of the methods described in Chapters 2 and 3 (see Figures 5, 6, and 7), it should generally have a focal length of at least 300 mm. This will show you the diamond ring, Baily's Beads, the prominences, and, of course, the corona. If you can get it, a system of longer focal length is generally preferable.

The longer the focal length, the greater the detail within your grasp—and there is a lot of detail. Of course, long-focal-length lenses have certain problems: Vibrations are magnified, and if you aren't careful camera shake can ruin the pictures; focusing must be exact; trailing, or blurring, due to the Earth's rotation becomes evident after a point; and, if the lens is too long, there won't be much room in the field of view for the corona. The longer the lens, the smaller the area it can "cover." A good all-purpose eclipse lens is in the neighborhood of 500 mm and has a field of view of about 2¾ × 4 degrees of angular size on 35-mm film, leaving room for about three and a half solar radii of corona.

For the Montana eclipse, I used a 5-cm (2-in.) refracting telescope coupled with a 35-mm single-lens-reflex camera body attached at prime focus with a homemade wooden brace. The 'scope had a focal length of 600 mm and proved to be ideal for just about all aspects of totality. By using the formula

$$\frac{700}{\text{Focal length of lens (in millimeters)}} = \text{maximum exposure time (in seconds)}$$

I figured I could take exposures of up to about one second before the apparent motion of the Sun would blur the image. I carefully planned out my exposure sequence well before leaving home and practiced it several times, cutting down the number of shots I wanted of totality until I managed to squeeze them all into 2 minutes 38 seconds, the time period I knew I would have, without too much trouble. The series I worked out went something like the scheme shown below.

All exposures are $f/12$ on Kodachrome 64 film, through thin hazy clouds.

Frame No.	.Exposure	Specific Target	Filter
1	1/30 sec	Uneclipsed Sun	Mylar, density 5
2–8	1/30 sec	Partial phase	Mylar, density 5
9	1/15 sec	Diamond ring	No filter
10	1/15 sec	Diamond ring	No filter
11	1/15 sec	Prominences	No filter
12	1/15 sec	Prominences	No filter
13	1/8 sec	Prominences	No filter
14	1/8 sec	Prominences	No filter
15	1/2 sec	Inner corona	No filter
16	1/2 sec	Inner corona	No filter
17	1/2 sec	Inner corona	No filter
18	1 sec	Middle corona	No filter
19	1 sec	Middle corona	No filter
20	4 sec	Middle corona	No filter
21	8 sec	Outer corona	No filter

Frame No.	Exposure	Specific Target	Filter
22	1/125 sec	3rd Contact/ Prominences	No filter
23	1/125 sec	3rd Contact/ Prominences	No filter
24	1/125 sec	Diamond ring	No filter

I am sure that if I hadn't practiced my routine, things wouldn't have gone nearly so smoothly as they did. As it was, almost half the shots of totality were ruined by vibrations. I learned the hard way how essential it is to let every shake of the telescope die down after winding the film and cocking the shutter. It's not worth taking a great many shots if none of them come out; take your time and make sure the pictures you do take are the best you can make them.

During the excitement of totality Murphy's Law manifests itself; that is, if anything can go wrong, it will. Things happen very fast during a total eclipse; you must decide well in advance what you are going to look for and what you are going to photograph. Know your routine, be familiar with your equipment, focus carefully, let every bit of vibration die down between shots, and your chances of getting photos you'll be proud of will be greatly multiplied.

I also strongly recommend keeping careful records of *every* sky photograph you take. This includes all technical information—such as exposure time, film type, aperture, *f*/ratio, lens focal length—as well as any comments you think are important. This way, you'll be able to repeat or improve on your good shots and avoid repeating any mistakes.

CHAPTER 2

· ·

EXPLORING THE STARS

Perhaps now is a good time to backtrack to some more basic material. A reasonable starting point is stellar photography, since the techniques involved apply to most other sky-photography subjects, as well.

If, on a given night, you spot a certain star and come back to it in an hour or so, it will have moved noticeably. Indeed, as the night wears on, all the stars will appear to drift slowly in giant circles from east to west for the same reason the Sun and the Moon rise and set: As Earth rotates daily on its axis, all celestial objects seem to move in the opposite direction, eventually setting, rising again, and returning to the same position, all in approximately twenty-four hours. You can show this apparent motion of the stars on film with the simplest of equipment: a camera, a cable release, and a tripod.

Star trails are the easiest nighttime subjects. By merely leaving the camera shutter open, with the camera pointed at any area of the night sky, you can record the motion of each star in the form of a circular arc. The longer you leave the shutter open, the more each star will have moved, and thus the lengthier each "trail" will be. The camera must have a provision for holding the shutter open for a long period of time. Many cameras have a connection point for a cable release and a "B" (for *bulb*) designation on the shutter-speed selector dial, for use in time exposures as well as flash-bulb exposures. Most instant-loading cameras, unfortunately, cannot be used for time exposures.

To make the star-trail photograph, set the camera on the tripod facing the stars or constellation you wish to capture on film. Make sure no unwanted lights are shining on the camera and open the shutter, locking it open with the cable-release lock.

You can leave the shutter open as long as you like. Generally, the longer the trails, the more interesting and beautiful they are. There are, however, a few limits to the length of the exposure. The obvious one, of course, is the coming of predawn twilight—if dawn breaks before the shutter is closed, the picture will look washed out.

Not so obvious, however, is the problem of sky fog. That is, the longer you expose, the lighter the background in the photograph becomes until eventually the stars can no longer be seen. The limit of exposure time varies with the sensitivity of the film used, the "speed," or *f*/ratio, of the lens you are using, and the lightness of the background sky. A "fast" lens system—one with a low *f*/ratio—will fog the picture sooner than a "slow" lens. The fog limit can be anywhere from twenty minutes or so to several hours. You will have to experiment to find the fog limit of your own system. You can increase exposure time by closing the lens opening (stopping down) to provide a higher *f*/ratio. All this does, though, is to give your lens a smaller aperture, and that means that dimmer stars will not register on the film's emulsion, or sensitive layer. You will get longer star trails, thanks to the longer exposures, but you'll get fewer stars. (For a description of *f*/ratios, check Appendix I.)

Try using color film for star trails; the different stars will leave trails of different hues and brightnesses, creating a striking image.

It is particularly interesting to turn your camera to the region of Polaris, the North Star. Earth's axis of rotation points toward one spot in space, and in a photograph all the stars seem to revolve around that one point, near Polaris. A star-trail picture of the region—called a polar trail—will show that Polaris itself is not exactly centered on the celestial pole (see Figure 11 in Appendix I) but makes a tiny arc around that point, the center of all the star-trail circles.

Star trails leave plenty of room for artistry. You can incorporate city skylines, landscapes, trees, or any other earthly subjects with a portion of the sky in a single photo. Also, you can never be sure exactly what will happen during the exposure. Once when I got back a set of slides from the film processor I had a great deal of trouble figuring out what the bright green dots in my polar-trail photo were. Little had I realized that during the five-hour exposure several fireflies had meandered through the field of view, leaving their trails, too, on the film for posterity.

Star trails are fine if all you want to do is show the apparent motion of the stars and the bright planets. But what if you want true images of the stars, a point for each one? Then you must move the camera in such a way that it follows the stars as they wheel across the sky. Each star will then show up in the photograph as a point of light rather than a curved streak. This technique is known as *clock driving*.

Clock-driven time exposures are of especial importance to the astronomer and astrophotographer because in them the special characteristic of photographic film known as reciprocity comes into play. The Law of Reciprocity states that the density of the image on the film is in direct proportion to the length of exposure. In other words, the longer you expose the film, the more the light from the subject will affect the emulsion, or sensitive layer of the film. This means that things like dim galaxies, clusters of stars, and clouds of glowing gas that are invisible to the eye even through giant telescopes will show up in a photograph—provided that the film is exposed for long enough.

It is also because of reciprocity, of course, that by varying the shutter speed of the camera for a picture, be it terrestrial or celestial, one can obtain a proper exposure. For example, 1/250 sec might be too short an exposure for, say, the Moon photographed with a given setup—there just wouldn't be time for the light to have a strong enough effect on the film. But perhaps 1/125 sec would do the trick: Twice the total amount of light would get through to the film, and so you would get an image of the right brightness. Likewise, when you expose while using a clock drive, what you are doing is moving the camera along with the celestial objects so as to allow the light from each star to form an increasingly dense spot on the film as the exposure progresses in time.

Tracking the stars is not as easy as it might sound. The simple *altazimuth* telescope mount, which has up-and-down motion on one axis (altitude) and side-to-side motion on the other (azimuth) (see Figure 3), is not really practical here. To track a ce-

Figure 3.   AN ALTAZIMUTH MOUNT can move only up and down (altitude) and side to side (azimuth). Both motions are required to track celestial objects, such as the star rising in the diagram.

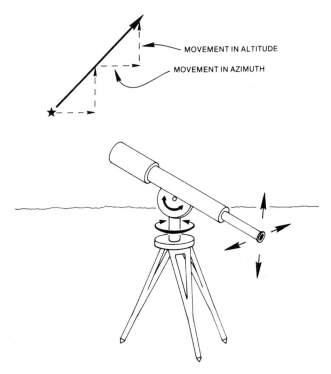

MOVEMENT IN ALTITUDE

MOVEMENT IN AZIMUTH

lestial object with an altazimuth-mounted telescope, you have to move the instrument on both axes—up and across, up and across, like a staircase. This does not lend itself to long-exposure photography, or even to serious observing, because it is often difficult to coordinate the two motions. Above all, it would be nearly impossible to clock-drive an altazimuth mount because motors would be needed on both axes and at ever-changing rates as the object wheeled across the sky. What we need is an instrument mount with a *single* axis around which we can rotate the instrument in pursuit of the stars. Such an axis is provided in a special type of mount, the *equatorial.*

The idea behind an equatorial mount is this: One axis, the *polar axis,* is parallel with the axis of the Earth. As Earth spins from west to east, the stars seem to drift in the opposite direction. A telescope or camera mounted on an equatorial mount need only be turned slowly on the polar axis to follow the subject. It is a simple, accurate motion, and one far superior to the stair steps of an altazimuth mount.

One of the most popular types of equatorial mounts is the German equatorial (see Figure 4), which is used on a great many amateur and professional telescopes. This type has a *declination* axis at right angles to the polar axis. There is a shaft along the declination axis to which the viewing instrument is attached. As with all equatorials, you find the object you wish to see or photograph by turning the telescope or camera on both axes. Then, once you have the object centered, you guide the instrument around the polar axis at a speed that will keep the object in view. (For more detail on celestial motions, see *Coordinates in the Sky* in Appendix I.)

The least your equatorial mount should have is some sort of gearing system, so that you can move the camera manually with reasonable accuracy. Often a hand-turned knob controls the driving gears. Most amateur and virtually all professional instruments, however, have electric clock drives to turn the instrument at the appropriate speed around the polar axis. If you plan to take only wide-angle photographs with lenses of short focal lengths, the mount and drive system need not be extravagant. But if you will be using long-focal-length lenses or per-

Figure 4. A GERMAN EQUATORIAL MOUNT. As the earth rotates from west to east, the stars seem to rotate in the opposite direction. Turning the telescope around the polar axis will counteract this apparent motion and so permit perfect tracking of a star.

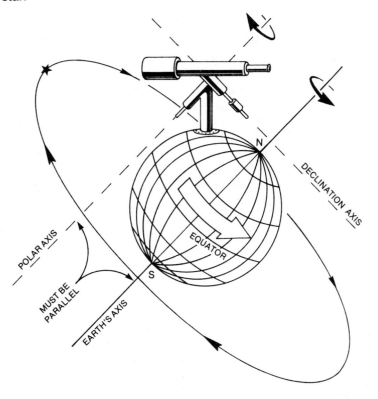

haps even a telescope for photography, the mount will have to be solid and smooth-turning, and the drive, accurate and smooth.

For now, let's assume you are using fairly modest equipment, for example a 35-mm camera and a lens of standard focal length, such as 50 mm. (For 35-mm cameras, lenses of about 45 mm to 58 mm are considered normal.) With a lens of this length you can cover a good portion of the sky in a single frame. The 50-degree diagonal coverage of this focal length is adequate for most constellations and is certainly enough to show a good stretch of the Milky Way. The question is: How are you going to make sure that you (or the electric clock drive) are tracking at the right speed?

It depends on your setup. One popular method is the *piggyback,* in which the camera is strapped to the side of an equatorially mounted telescope. (It is usually not too hard to attach the camera to the side of the telescope, as the tripod socket on most cameras is a standard thread, 1/4 × 20. I made a simple wooden platform to strap to the tube of my 6-in. reflector with a 1/4 × 20 bolt that goes through the platform. A knob on one end of the bolt helps turn the bolt to tighten the camera to the platform. Alternatively, there are commercial holders available.) With the camera shutter open, you look through the eyepiece of the telescope at a single star, all the while making sure it stays in the same position.

In the piggyback setup, the telescope's optics are not used for the photograph at all; you are just making use of the equatorial mount and clock drive to support and guide the camera. Since the 50-mm lens doesn't require extreme accuracy, it is often enough to locate a guide star at the edge of the eyepiece field of view, for reference. If the star starts to move toward the center of the field of view, or if it goes out of sight, you must speed up or slow down the tracking motion to keep pace with it. If you are tracking manually, this is done by merely turning the control knob faster or more slowly. If you have an electric clock drive, the most common method is to plug it into an electronic drive-corrector, drawing power from a household outlet or a car battery. Controls on the drive-corrector allow you to change the telescope's tracking speed by small amounts.

Sometimes, if the equatorial mount has been set up carefully with regard to the celestial pole, if the drive is very accurate, and if you are using a short-focal-length lens on the camera, you can leave the camera unattended for a minute or so; but usually you should guide it constantly.

Exposure times for clock-driven photography can run from a few minutes to more than an hour. This might easily spell serious trouble for your back and neck—you really have to stay glued to the eyepiece, often bent over in precarious and painful positions. You'll make things much easier on yourself by bringing some sort of chair out to the telescope; I use a high kitchen stool. Another hint for easing the strain of long exposures: music to keep you company.

When accurate guiding is needed, a useful accessory is a cross-hair eyepiece for the guide telescope. With this device, it is easier to keep track of the guide star than using the edge-of-the-view method. A more extravagant version of the cross-hair eyepiece is the illuminated-reticle eyepiece, which shows a grid and has a battery-operated lamp for better visibility against the dark sky.

As the telescope eases along with the stars, the camera, of course, moves along with it, and as a result the light from each star is concentrated on a single spot on the film.

Guiding can have other difficulties. The longer the focal length of the camera lens you are using, the more small imperfections in guiding will show up, and so the more carefully you must guide to get good results. If the mount is not aligned precisely with the celestial pole, you can make endless corrections in right ascension (the celestial equivalent of earthly longitude—see Glossary) and still not be able to follow the stars accurately; what you need is some mechanical way to correct in declination, too (that's the celestial equivalent of terrestrial latitude). This can often be done manually, sometimes electrically. Many declination slow-motion controls consist of gear combinations similar to clock drives found on many polar shafts, but there are other types suited to different types of equipment.

You can use the piggyback method for lenses from wide-angle to moderate telephoto, perhaps 500 mm or so. The instrument you are using for guiding should always be at least a little more powerful than the lens with which you are shooting; otherwise, guiding errors you can't even see through the guide 'scope eyepiece will show up in the photograph. A useful rule of thumb for guide-telescope magnification is

$$M = \frac{\textit{F.L. of photo-taking lens (in mm)}}{12}$$

For example, if you were shooting through a lens with a F.L. (focal length) of 500 mm, you would need a guide 'scope of at least

$$\frac{500}{12} = 42$$

giving a 42× or 42-power magnification. This is a very general rule, however, and usually you would want the guide 'scope to be more powerful. Experiment to see what power magnification you need to achieve good star images. Remember that enlarging an original photograph magnifies guiding errors (see E.F.L. in the Glossary).

One common solution to the guide 'scope with too low a power is to add a Barlow lens to the guiding outfit. This is a negative (concave) lens that jacks up the power by a factor of two or three, allowing you to be more critical in your guiding. Fortunately, good optics are not absolutely necessary for a guide telescope.

The important thing to remember about star pictures is that it is the aperture, or diameter, of the picture-taking lens rather than its *f*/ratio that determines its light-gathering power with regard to stars. The stars, being so far away, are virtually point sources of light, and so the image on the film is virtually a point. A lens 3 cm in diameter and 6 cm in focal length (*f*/2) will not show any fainter stars than will a 3-cm lens of 12-cm focal length (*f*/4). Both lenses collect exactly the same amount of starlight and concentrate it in an image of the same size.

In mathematical terms, you might say that the light-gathering power of a lens for a point source increases in direct proportion to the square of its diameter. That is, if you double the diameter of a lens, you quadruple its "star power"; if you triple the diameter, you increase the power ninefold.

Table 3 shows approximately what magnitude of star you can expect to record using a lens of any of several diameters. The *magnitude* of a star is a measure of its brightness. The lower the magnitude, the brighter the object; the higher, the dimmer. Very bright stars have negative magnitudes, while the faintest stars visible to the naked eye are of about magnitude 6.5. Table 3 is only approximate and depends on such variables as film speed, sky conditions, and lens quality. (See *Aperture* in Glossary.)

Table 3. MAGNITUDE OF FAINTEST STAR

Exposure Time

Aperture of lens	1 min	3 min	9 min	27 min	90 min
25 mm	7.5	8.5	9.5	10.5	11.5
50 mm	9	10	11	12	13
75 mm	10	11	12	13	14
100 mm	10.5	11.5	12.5	13.5	14.5
150 mm	11.5	12.5	13.5	14.5	15.5
200 mm	12	13	14	15	16

Stars and constellations are not, by far, the only stellar objects for lens and camera. Some of the most interesting nighttime subjects, in fact, are the "open" and "globular" star clusters. The Pleiades, for example, is one of the most famous open clusters. Six or eight stars are easily visible to the naked eye, and dozens more are revealed through a telescope or a long-exposure photograph.

The Pleiades will show up in even a very short exposure with a short-focal-length lens. To show detail in the nebula surrounding the Pleiades, however, and to reveal the fainter stars of the cluster, you will want to move on to bigger equipment. Both larger aperture and longer focal length are needed. This is true with all open and globular clusters. Although some clusters, such as the Pleiades, are reasonably large (in angular measurement), most are quite small, and you will have to use long-focal-length lenses to have an image of reasonable size. A 50-mm lens yields an image of M 13, the famous Hercules cluster, of less than 0.2 mm.

Although the piggyback setup will sometimes work for star clusters if the photographic lens is a big one—for example, one of the retrofocus, or "mirror," lenses available for many 35-mm camera bodies—usually this is the point at which you must shoot through a telescope itself. Amateur telescopes used for stellar photography can be of all different kinds, but the most common ones are moderate-aperture *refracting* and *reflecting* telescopes.

The *prime focus* camera-telescope system is usually the best for stellar photography. The camera body, with lens removed, must be positioned at the telescope in such a way that the primary image from the telescope's objective (the main lens in a refractor or the main mirror in a reflector) is focused directly on the film (see Figure 5). There are several commercially available adapters to attach a camera body to a telescope's eyepiece-holder for prime-focus systems (see Figure 6). The eyepiece-holder itself is used to focus the image on the film. Sometimes the primary image in a reflecting telescope is too far inside to reach the film. In this case, the main mirror must be moved forward an inch or two in the telescope.

Because the long focal lengths involved require highly accurate focusing, reflex viewing on the camera is essential.

In photographing through the telescope, you will need a different method for guiding than with the piggyback system. The more popular solution is to mount another telescope, usually a smaller one, directly onto the main tube of the bigger instrument. With the camera attached to the eyepiece-holder of the big 'scope, you guide through the smaller one, which is preferably equipped with a cross-hair eyepiece.

Quite often, you will need a Barlow lens to increase the power of the guide 'scope—this will depend on the effective focal length (E.F.L.) of the main picture-taking telescope. This is the focal length a simple lens would need in order to produce images of the same size as your system will produce. Remember that if you plan to enlarge the original photograph, you will be increasing the E.F.L. In practice, this means that a 3 × 5–in. print from a negative made on 35-mm film is a roughly 3× enlargement, from 24 × 36 mm to about 75 × 125 mm. This effectively increases the E.F.L. by three times—but in the darkroom, not in the telescope.

The other common method of guiding a telescope-camera system in long-exposure photography is the *off-axis* method. An off-axis guiding system intercepts a small, usually insignificant, portion of the light in the main 'scope's eyepiece focuser before it reaches the film, sending it instead to an eyepiece through which the observer can watch during the exposure.

Although some off-axis systems are quite expensive, they are considerably lighter in weight than a separate guide 'scope, and they have the added advantage of letting you see exactly what you will get in the photograph. A guide 'scope must be carefully aligned parallel with the main instrument in order to show you exactly what the camera is "seeing." A disadvantage

Figure 5.   PRIME-FOCUS SYSTEMS. In (a) and (b), the primary images from the objectives of refracting and reflecting telescopes, respectively, are focused directly on the film. In (c), 35-mm S.L.R. camera body (1) is mounted on a reflecting telescope for prime-focus photography, and fitted with a locking cable release (2). The main telescope's spotting scope is at (3).

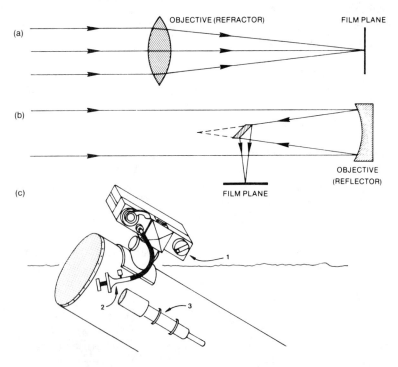

Figure 6. A CAMERA ADAPTER and a TELESCOPE EYE-PIECE. Part A attaches directly to a camera body. Part C slides into the telescope's eyepiece focuser. For prime focus, parts A and C are used alone. For positive projection (see Chapter 3), parts A, B, and C are all used with an eyepiece inserted.

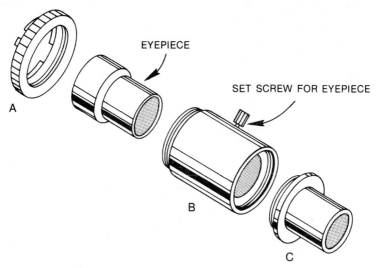

of off-axis guiding systems, by the same token, is that occasionally you will get stuck with a dim guide star, making guiding difficult, whereas a separate guide 'scope can always be adjusted so as to center on a bright guide star.

A clock drive with a slow-motion control and usually a slow motion in declination, too, are musts, because you will be using lenses of long focal lengths, and these need precise guiding corrections.

Although some clusters, such as the Pleiades, are quite bright, many are dim and need fairly long exposures—an hour or more for a globular cluster is not uncommon.

Many films can be used successfully for shooting open and globular clusters. The only general rule of thumb is that they be "fast"—that is, very sensitive. Color transparency ("slide") films make for beautiful pictures, but some black-and-white films may offer more speed and resolution.

During such extralong exposures as those needed for star clusters a curious phenomenon known as *reciprocity failure* comes into play. This is a film characteristic that continues to plague astrophotographers. As an exposure progresses in time, photographic film becomes increasingly insensitive to light and the Law of Reciprocity (referred to at the beginning of this section) fails to hold. Instead, a film's sensitivity may decrease during long exposure from a capability of, say, ISO 400 to virtually zero. After a certain point, in other words, it doesn't pay to expose a shot any longer; you would just be wasting your time. Thus, reciprocity-law failure must be taken into account when you are calculating correct exposure.

Suppose, for example, you wish to duplicate a correctly exposed shot of an open star cluster. The original was taken with a telescope of 14-cm aperture and exposed for half an hour. If the second shot is to be taken with a 10-cm-aperture instrument (about half the light-gathering power as the original with respect to stars), it would appear that you need merely expose the shot for twice as long as the original, or one hour—assuming you are using the same type and sensitivity of film. But throughout that hour the sensitivity of the film has been dropping off constantly, until during the last half-hour it is functioning at a much lower sensitivity than during the first half-hour. This means that merely doubling the exposure time of the original to compensate for the smaller aperture is not enough. Instead, you must expose even longer—perhaps ten or twenty minutes, or even more, depending on the reciprocity characteristics of the particular film you are using. This is one reason manufacturers like Eastman Kodak make specialized astrophotography films.

In color films, reciprocity failure usually affects different colors by different amounts, so that long exposures often take on hues slightly shifted from normal.

SUMMARY

Star Trails

EQUIPMENT: Camera, locking cable release, sturdy tripod
  Optics: Short-focal-length lens (wide-angle to normal); *f*/ra-

tio—whatever available, or whatever needed to allow desired trail length without reaching the sky-fog limit
EXPOSURE: As long as desired; any exposure longer than

$$\frac{700}{E.F.L. \ (in \ mm)} \ sec$$

will show a trail
FILM: Anything will do.

Clock-Driven Targets

EQUIPMENT: Camera, locking cable release, equatorial mount, some method of guiding (piggyback, off-axis, etc.)
Optics: To suit target—anywhere from wide-angle camera lenses for large stretches of sky to long-focal-length telescopes for star clusters (the larger the aperture, the better, in general)
EXPOSURE: The longer the exposure, the more stars you will capture, although you can't really expose all night (Table 3 shows approximate magnitude limitation to expect for various apertures)
FILM: The more sensitive, the better; daylight color transparency ("slide"), specialized spectroscopic black-and-white negative film—all will work.

CHAPTER 3

. . . .

LUNAR PHOTOGRAPHY

One evening while observing from New Mexico, I turned the 12-cm telescope toward the beautiful first-quarter Moon and bent down to the eyepiece hopefully. My jaw must have dropped as I looked head-on at a gigantic space-spider straddling the Moon, obviously about to jump the relatively small gap to Earth and take over the world. Applying my reasoning powers, I deduced that a tiny spider had found its way into the telescope eyepiece and spun a few strands of web there. It was suspended almost exactly at the focus point of the eyepiece, so that both it and the Moon were in focus at the same time. By the time I had returned with my camera, the spider had taken up residence inside the telescope itself, where it eventually died.

You can be quite sure you will never get a picture of a lunar spider. In fact, you will not even get pictures of the spacecraft left on the Moon after the Apollo missions, no matter how large your telescope. Yet you can be quite sure of being able to get some kind of satisfactory shot of the Moon with just about any lens-camera combination.

Our nearest neighbor in the solar system, the Moon appears relatively large—about half a degree across in angular measure—and is the second brightest object in our sky, at magnitude minus-twelve. These factors all make it one of the easiest targets for a camera aimed at the sky. Despite this, it will soon become apparent to an experimenter that lenses of short focal length just won't reveal any *detail* on the lunar surface. While you might get some beautiful moonscape shots with your normal lens or a moderate telephoto, you will generally be better off attaching the camera body to a telescope.

There are several ways to attach a camera to a telescope for lunar photography, but there are two major sorts: *projection* and *prime focus* (which is also used for star photography, as described in the previous chapter). For prime focus, you must somehow affix the camera so that the primary image of the telescope falls on the film. The telescope itself then actually functions as a sort of supertelephoto lens.

There are several simple commercial camera adapters that will attach a camera body to a telescope's eyepiece focuser, with an eyepiece in place (for the projection method) or without one (for the prime-focus method) (see Figure 6). Thus, the eyepiece focuser can be used to move the camera in and out until the image on the ground-glass focusing screen is good and sharp. Because of the long focal lengths usually involved, focusing is critical; a ground-glass focusing screen, such as that in a 35-mm or larger reflex camera, is a must, and a high-powered magnifying eyepiece at the camera viewfinder is certainly a big help.

Projection methods can be further divided into three parts: *afocal* projection, eyepiece projection *(positive),* and Barlow projection *(negative).*

The *afocal* method should really be saved for cameras whose lenses cannot be removed. It involves more lenses than any other telescope-camera combination, and this almost always spells trouble for image quality. In this method, both the eyepiece of the telescope *and* the normal camera lens are left in place. The eyepiece is focused at infinity, so that light rays from any given point on the subject leave the eyepiece in parallel "bundles." The camera lens, also focused at infinity, functions just as it would for a normal distant daytime object, collecting the parallel light rays and focusing them on the film. The end product is an image on the film enlarged from the primary image made by the telescope objective (see Figure 7).

The first step is some sort of sturdy holder to keep the camera steadily aligned with the eyepiece. This can be either bought or made out of wood or metal. In general, it is handy to have a holder that can pivot in several directions so that the camera can be positioned easily. Although an eyepiece in focus for visual use is theoretically in focus for the afocal system, you really can't afford just to attach the camera to the eyepiece blindly. At such great focal lengths, reflex focusing is completely necessary.

The next step is to decide how far away the camera lens should be from the telescope eyepiece. The distance will not affect focusing, but only the amount of light reaching the film—naturally, the more light, the better. The point is that you must locate the exit pupil of the telescope as near as possible to the *diaphragm* of the camera. The exit pupil is the point outside the eyepiece of a telescope where the emerging light rays are most concentrated. To do this, point the telescope at the sky or a white wall and move the camera, in its place at the eyepiece, back and forth until the entire viewfinder is illuminated evenly.

The effective focal length and the f/ratios of the system can be found by the formulas below. By having the focal length of the camera lens longer than that of the eyepiece, you will have as your final image a magnified version of the primary image. If you use a 50-mm lens with a 25-mm eyepiece, for instance, the original image will be magnified twice (2×). A long-focal-length camera lens and/or a short-focal-length eyepiece will give you higher *projection magnification.*

AFOCAL CALCULATIONS

$$Projection\ magnification\ (P.M.) = \frac{\text{Camera focal length (F.L.)}}{\text{Eyepiece focal length (F.L.)}}$$

Effective focal length (E.F.L.) = Telescope objective F.L. × P.M.

OR

$$E.F.L. = Power\ of\ telescope \times Camera\ F.L.$$

$$f/Ratio = \frac{E.F.L.}{Telescope\ aperture\ (A.)}$$

OR

$$f/Ratio = f/Ratio\ of\ telescope \times P.M.$$

Figure 7. THE THREE PROJECTION SYSTEMS. In all three cases, a camera body holds the film at the film plane. In the positive and negative systems, the distance D between the eyepiece (or negative lens) and the final image on the film is used in calculating projection magnification. Since most eyepieces have more than one lens, you can measure D from the center point between the eyepiece's two outside lenses. The camera lens is used only in the afocal system.

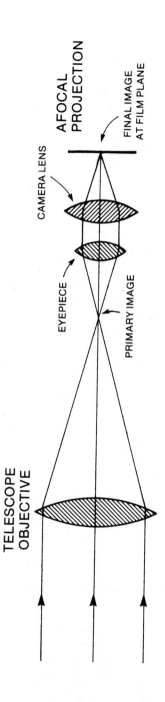

TELESCOPE
OBJECTIVE

EYEPIECE

PRIMARY IMAGE

CAMERA LENS

AFOCAL
PROJECTION

FINAL IMAGE
AT FILM PLANE

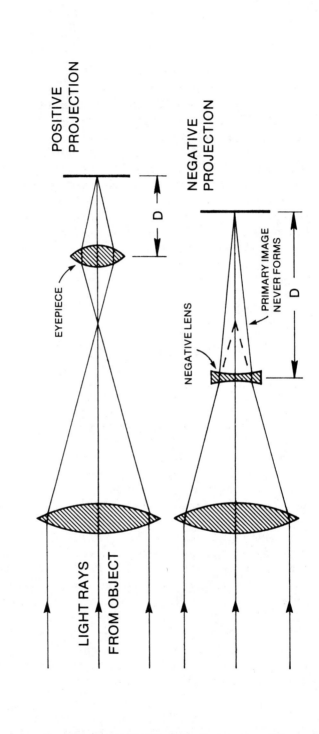

For *eyepiece* or *positive projection,* almost any telescope with the eyepiece extended a little from the normal position can be used. A camera body is needed, but no camera lens. The theory is simple: The primary image from the telescope objective, be it mirror or lens, is analagous to a slide in a projector. The eyepiece acts as the projector lens, throwing an enlarged secondary image of the first image onto the film, which functions as the viewing screen. Just as with a slide projector, the farther away the screen—in our case, the film—the larger the secondary image; by moving the camera farther out, you get a bigger picture on the "screen." At the same time, you have to move the eyepiece in, closer to the primary image, in order to keep the secondary image focused (see Figure 7). You can also get higher magnification by using a shorter-focal-length eyepiece.

POSITIVE PROJECTION CALCULATIONS

$$P.M. = \frac{D - (eyepiece\ F.L.)}{eyepiece\ F.L.} \quad (for\ D,\ see\ Figure\ 7)$$

$$E.F.L. = Telescope\ objective\ F.L. \times P.M.$$

$$f/Ratio = \frac{E.F.L.}{Telescope\ A.}$$

$$f/ratio = f/Ratio\ of\ telescope \times P.M.$$

Often the only problem with eyepiece projection is the mechanical coupling of camera to telescope eyepiece. Sometimes you can use the same type of external camera holder as for the afocal system; indeed, if the telescope's eyepiece holder is not very strong—as is often the case—you will need an external holder no matter what.

An easier method is to use the same type of commercially sold camera adapter as that used for prime-focus systems, shown in Figure 6. You just pop the eyepiece of your choice (depending on projection magnification desired) into the eyepiece part of the adapter, attach the adapter to the camera body, insert the adapter into the telescope's eyepiece holder-focuser, and use the last-named to focus the image through the camera viewfinder. Then, to find the projection magnification of your system, use the formula below.

For example, let's say you are using a 5-cm f/12 refracting telescope (F.L. = 50 mm × 12 = 600 mm). You are using a 10-mm eyepiece with a commercial camera adapter for eyepiece projection. You measure the value D of your adapter-camera-body combination (see Figure 7—the distance between the middle of the eyepiece and the film) as 80 mm. You calculate:

$$P.M. = \frac{80mm - 10mm}{10 \ mm} \doteq 7$$

$$E.F.L. = 600 \ mm \times 7 = 4200 \ mm$$

$$f/Ratio = \frac{4200mm}{50mm} = f/84$$

OR $f/Ratio = 12 \times 7 = f/84$.

The E.F.L. of 4200 mm will yield an image of the Full Moon almost 37 mm across (see *Focal length* in Appendix I for image-size formulas). This is a tiny bit larger than the long side of a 35-mm-film frame (24×36mm). The f/ratio calculated can be used to determine exposure times. For example, if you are using an ISO 125 film, you can see from the lunar-exposure graph (Table 4) that for f/90—the f/ratio on the graph closest to f/84—a proper exposure for the Crescent Moon would be about 16 seconds.

Negative lens projection is based on use of the Barlow lens, a negative lens inserted in the optical path *before* the primary image is formed (see Figure 7). This creates an enlarged image focused farther from the objective than the original was. One advantage of negative lens projection is its compactness. With a negative lens you can achieve the same degree of projection magnification as with a positive lens system, but in a much smaller space and with the camera body a good deal closer to the telescope. It is often easier to manage than the positive lens system and requires a little less counterbalancing of the telescope.

NEGATIVE PROJECTION CALCULATIONS

Calculations for negative lens systems are the same as for positive systems, except that

$$P.M. = \frac{D + (negative \ lens \ F.L.)}{negative \ lens \ F.L.}$$

No matter what system you use in photographing the Moon, beyond a certain minimum focal length practically any camera-telescope combination will give you some sort of satisfactory picture.

A typical modest outfit might include a refracting telescope with an aperture of a few centimeters, or a small reflector. Either could be used at prime focus. A focal length of 600 mm will yield an image of the Moon about 5.5 mm across (see Appendix I, under *Focal length,* for image-size formulas). This will give a good view of the phase of the Moon at the time and will show the maria, the dark, relatively smooth areas or "seas," or the Moon's surface. At double that length (1200 mm) the lunar image is about 11 mm across, which is close to half the height of the 35-mm film frame. This focal length will show a good bit of detail in the Moon's craters, especially if the Moon is at first or third quarter. Then the day/night line (the *terminator*) is side-lighted from our point of view.

The longest focal length you can use and still fit the Full Moon's entire image onto a 35-mm frame (with a little room to spare) is about 2500 mm—some hundred inches. For example, this focal length can be reached by using a 15.2 cm (6 in.) f/8 reflecting telescope and the eyepiece projection method to provide a projection magnification of about 2×.

As you continue to jack up the E.F.L. of your system using positive or negative projection systems, you begin to zero in on detail on the lunar surface. Tiny craters begin to show up, mountain ranges are sharply seen. It is at these superlong focal lengths, however, that the going gets rough. The longer the focal length, the more tiny shakes and vibrations, such as those caused by a breeze, will show up in the picture in the form of a double or blurred image.

One major cause of camera vibration is the quick snap-back of the mirror in a single-lens-reflex camera. To eliminate this problem, a few cameras have mirror locks. After advancing the film and focusing and composing the image, you lock up the mirror, let the telescope stop vibrating and settle down, and release the shutter by means of a cable release. The only camera-made vibration then will be the relatively small one caused by the opening and closing of the shutter itself. Even this miniscule vibration might be enough to ruin a shot, though, especially if you are using extremely high projection magnification.

Generally, by jacking up the E.F.L. by so much you are also increasing the focal ratio. This, in turn, means longer and longer exposures are necessary, often a few seconds or more. Yet this in turn can pave the way for a method that eliminates the effect of camera vibration: While holding a piece of black cardboard in front of the telescope, press the cable release and lock it to hold the shutter open. When the vibrations die down, take the cardboard away for the required exposure time—say, 4 seconds—then move the cardboard back to block the moonlight from the telescope and close the shutter.

The Moon's brightness often allows fast shutter speeds, meaning that you won't always need a clock drive. By the same token, an equatorial mount, although certainly convenient, is not always necessary. If you don't have a clock drive, you must stick to fast films and/or fast (low) focal ratios because the long exposure required by slow films or high f/ratios would allow time for the Moon to drift noticeably.

The problem of drift increases rapidly as the focal length increases. Not only is Earth's motion more apparent at longer focal lengths but also, by increasing the E.F.L. of a given telescope (by eyepiece projection, for instance), you also increase the focal ratio and so make longer exposures necessary. These two phenomena combine to reach a point where a clock-driven equatorial mount is needed and, after that, more and more accurate driving. Use the graph in Table 4 to estimate exposure times (see example given for positive projection method, p. 59).

While the Full Moon does evoke a good bit of ancient mystique, it is generally the least interesting lunar phase as a subject for an astrocamera. Because the Sun is virtually directly behind the observer of the Full Moon, the lighting is flat—no shadows are cast. True, the ray structures radiating from some of the craters (Tycho, for instance) can be seen best during the Full Moon, but when the craters and mountain ranges are lighted from directly above, they cast no shadows, making for generally dull pictures compared with phases when the Sun's light

Table 4

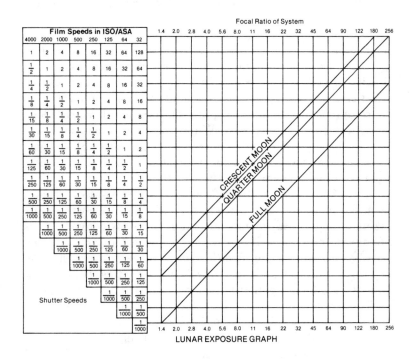

Focal Ratio of System

Film Speeds in ISO/ASA							
4000	2000	1000	500	250	125	64	32
1	2	4	8	16	32	64	128
$\frac{1}{2}$	1	2	4	8	16	32	64
$\frac{1}{4}$	$\frac{1}{2}$	1	2	4	8	16	32
$\frac{1}{8}$	$\frac{1}{4}$	$\frac{1}{2}$	1	2	4	8	16
$\frac{1}{15}$	$\frac{1}{8}$	$\frac{1}{4}$	$\frac{1}{2}$	1	2	4	8
$\frac{1}{30}$	$\frac{1}{15}$	$\frac{1}{8}$	$\frac{1}{4}$	$\frac{1}{2}$	1	2	4
$\frac{1}{60}$	$\frac{1}{30}$	$\frac{1}{15}$	$\frac{1}{8}$	$\frac{1}{4}$	$\frac{1}{2}$	1	2
$\frac{1}{125}$	$\frac{1}{60}$	$\frac{1}{30}$	$\frac{1}{15}$	$\frac{1}{8}$	$\frac{1}{4}$	$\frac{1}{2}$	1
$\frac{1}{250}$	$\frac{1}{125}$	$\frac{1}{60}$	$\frac{1}{30}$	$\frac{1}{15}$	$\frac{1}{8}$	$\frac{1}{4}$	$\frac{1}{2}$
$\frac{1}{500}$	$\frac{1}{250}$	$\frac{1}{125}$	$\frac{1}{60}$	$\frac{1}{30}$	$\frac{1}{15}$	$\frac{1}{8}$	$\frac{1}{4}$
$\frac{1}{1000}$	$\frac{1}{500}$	$\frac{1}{250}$	$\frac{1}{125}$	$\frac{1}{60}$	$\frac{1}{30}$	$\frac{1}{15}$	$\frac{1}{8}$
	$\frac{1}{1000}$	$\frac{1}{500}$	$\frac{1}{250}$	$\frac{1}{125}$	$\frac{1}{60}$	$\frac{1}{30}$	$\frac{1}{15}$
		$\frac{1}{1000}$	$\frac{1}{500}$	$\frac{1}{250}$	$\frac{1}{125}$	$\frac{1}{60}$	$\frac{1}{30}$
			$\frac{1}{1000}$	$\frac{1}{500}$	$\frac{1}{250}$	$\frac{1}{125}$	$\frac{1}{60}$
				$\frac{1}{1000}$	$\frac{1}{500}$	$\frac{1}{250}$	$\frac{1}{125}$
Shutter Speeds					$\frac{1}{1000}$	$\frac{1}{500}$	$\frac{1}{250}$
						$\frac{1}{1000}$	$\frac{1}{500}$
							$\frac{1}{1000}$

Focal Ratio scale: 1.4　2.0　2.8　4.0　5.6　8.0　11　16　22　32　45　64　90　122　180　256

CRESCENT MOON / QUARTER MOON / FULL MOON

LUNAR EXPOSURE GRAPH

hits the lunar surface at an angle. First and third quarters are the times when the Moon seems to hold endless numbers of craters, mountain peaks, "rilles," or thin, wavy channels, and other features. Along the terminator, the line where bright and dark sides meet, these mountains and craters cast long shadows on the side away from the Sun; they seem to stand out in stark relief, conveying a true sense of the depth, height, and ruggedness of the lunar features.

It is often interesting to close in with the camera on small areas of the terminator, aiming for detail and resolution. The amount of detail you can record depends on the "seeing" (the clarity and steadiness of the air), on the aperture of the instrument you are using (the larger, the better), the care with which you focus, the resolution of the film you use, and the accuracy of your driving system. Focusing should be done on as dim a star as you can see in the viewfinder—this allows a more careful focus than is possible with a bright star. Take your time focusing. Bad focus is at least as likely as any of a host of other possible problems to ruin an astrophotograph, especially when you are using long-to-superlong focal lengths.

Lunar eclipses often provide beautiful targets for an astrophotographer. Lunar eclipses occur when the Moon, traveling in its orbit around the Earth, passes into Earth's penumbra (a penumbral lunar eclipse), part of the Earth's umbra (a partial lunar eclipse), or entirely into the umbra (a total lunar eclipse). There is none of the excitement of solar eclipses here, however. Total lunar eclipses can last more than six hours from beginning to end, with totality lasting up to 1 hour 40 minutes. Over these long stretches of time the Moon very gradually becomes dimmed as it passes through the Earth's penumbra, then into the darker umbra, and then out again in reverse order.

Equipment for lunar eclipse photography should generally show the whole Moon in the picture; refracting or reflecting telescopes with a camera body at prime focus are ideal. Or you could try the multiple-exposure method used for solar eclipses (see p. 32). No filter is used here, of course.

The Moon's color during totality is usually a deep amber or pink. This hue comes from sunlight, bent and reddened by the Earth's atmosphere, that strikes the Moon indirectly. Fast color films are recommended to capture it.

Exposure times are usually very difficult to estimate because the darkness of lunar eclipses varies tremendously from one to another; sometimes the totally eclipsed Moon all but disappears from sight, while sometimes it is plainly visible. For example, if you were using ISO 400 film and a telescope at $f/8$, exposures for mid-totality might be anywhere from 1 second for a bright eclipse to 1 minute for a dim one.

Aside from the total lunar eclipses and moonrise or moonset, there isn't much color on the Moon. In addition, color films usually have less fine resolution than do black-and-white films of the same sensitivity. It is therefore generally a good idea to stick to the black-and-white emulsions for Moon pictures. If your equipment has an equatorial mount with a clock drive, you can use the slower high-resolution films. Otherwise, you'll have to stick to fast films that permit short exposures and thus reduce trailing or blurring during the exposure.

SUMMARY

EQUIPMENT: Camera, locking cable release, telephoto lens or telescope

Optics: Focal length to suit specific target (Moon phase, specific craters, etc.)—about 300 mm is good starting point for detail; aperture as large as available—big aperture yields detail and low f/ratio; use prime focus, afocal, or positive or negative projection system to couple camera with telescope; reflex focusing on camera

Equatorial mount with clock-drive is desirable, though not always necessary

EXPOSURE: From graph in Table 4; varies with phase, f/ratio, and film speed

FILM: Just about anything will work, although fine-grain high-resolution films are best; use fast films if you have no clock drive.

TOTAL SOLAR ECLIPSE in Montana, Feb. 26, 1979. The coronal transient (two o'clock position) and the tremendous prominences of this particular eclipse are visible here. 1/15 sec on Kodachrome 64 film through thin hazy skies; F.L. 600 mm; *f*/12; A (aperture) 50 mm; prime focus of the 5-cm refractor.

THE DIAMOND RING of third contact brings totality of the Montana eclipse to an end. 1/125 sec, same equipment as previous photo.

STAR TRAILS. During this 5-hour exposure of the North Polar region, fireflies flew by, leaving their green dots of light in the picture. 5 hours on Fujichrome 100 film; F.L. 50 mm; *f*/1.8; lens and camera.

STAR TRAILS. An airplane flew by (dotted straight line) and I did some observing at the telescope during this shot. The red light I use showed up as the tangled red line in the foreground, as I bent down to consult star charts and stood up at the 'scope. 3½ hours on Kodachrome 64 film; F.L. 50 mm; *f*/1.8; lens and camera.

THE MILKY WAY in the constellation Cygnus. Only a small fraction of the stars in this relatively short exposure are visible to the naked eye. Guided for 10 min on Ektachrome 400 film; F.L. 50 mm; *f*/1.8; A (aperture) 28 mm; lens and camera.

TWO METEORS from the annual Perseid meteor shower flash through the summer Milky Way. The fainter one is to the upper right of center, heading for center. Guided for 20 min on Fujichrome 400 film; F.L. 50 mm; *f*/1.8; A 25 mm; lens and camera.

THE PLEIADES, open star cluster. Guided for 20 min on Koda-chrome 64 film; F.L. 270 mm; f/5.6; A 48 mm; lens and camera.

NEBULAE in Sagittarius. This view of the Southern Milky Way shows dozens of well-known objects, such as the Lagoon Neb-ula (lower left) and the Omega Nebula (top). Guided for 30 min on Fujichrome 100 film; F.L. 135 mm; f/2.8; A 48 mm; lens and camera.

THE CRESCENT MOON AND VENUS set soon after the Sun behind the New Jersey skyline. ¼ sec. on Fujichrome 100 film; F.L. 50 mm; f/1.8; A 28 mm; lens and camera.

THE FULL MOON during a PARTIAL LUNAR ECLIPSE. Here the umbra, the darkest part of the Earth's shadow, darkens part of the Moon. 1/250 sec on Fujichrome 400 film; F.L. 1220 mm; f/8; A 152 mm; prime focus of my 15.2 cm reflecting telescope.

THE "NEW MOON IN THE OLD MOON'S ARMS", a monthly phenomenon, is not an eclipse. Here the Crescent is illuminated directly by the Sun, while the rest of the Moon is dimly lighted by sunlight bouncing off the Earth. Clock-driven; 16 sec on Fujichrome 100 film; F.L. 1220 mm; f/8; A 152 mm; prime focus of the 15.2 cm reflector.

THE FIRST-QUARTER MOON shows a wealth of crater detail. Clock-driven; ⅛ sec on Kodachrome 64 film; F.L. 1220 mm; *f*/8; A 152 mm; prime focus of the 15.2 cm reflector.

THE LUNAR CRATER COPERNICUS and surrounding areas. Long F.L. and long exposure show the effects of bad seeing. Clock-driven; 16 sec on Plus-X film; F.L. 23,000 mm; *f*/152; A 152 mm; 19x eyepiece projection with 15.2 cm reflector.

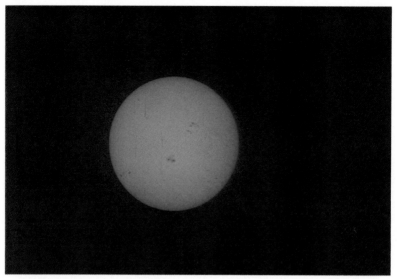

THE SUN, photographed through a sheet of aluminized Mylar, density 5. Limb darkening and several large sunspot groups can be seen here. 1/500 sec on Fujichrome 400 film; F.L. 1220 mm; f/8; A 152 mm; prime focus of the 15.2 cm reflector.

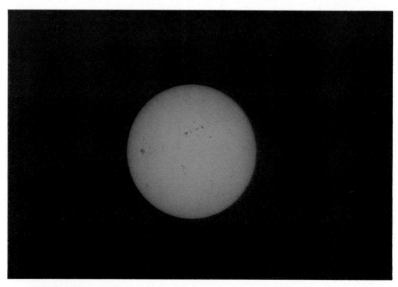

FOUR DAYS LATER, the Sun's rotation has carried the sunspots across the Sun's face. Same data as for previous photo.

JUPITER. Major cloud bands and some smaller details can be
seen here on the surface of the solar system's largest planet.
Clock-driven; 8 sec on Kodachrome 64 film; F.L. 23,000 mm;
$f/152$; A 152 mm; 19x eyepiece projection with 15.2 cm reflector.

VENUS in crescent phase. 1 sec on Plus-X film, exposed by hand with a piece of black cardboard; yellow (K2) filter for extra contrast; same setup as shot of Jupiter.

SATURN, replete with rings and some surface bands. Clock-driven; 2 sec on Ilford HP5 (ISO 400) film; F.L. 18,000 mm; *f*/90; A 203 mm; 6x eyepiece projection with 20.3 cm refractor.

M 42, THE ORION NEBULA. Slightly off-round star images are tell-tale signs of guiding errors. Guided for 20 min on Ilford HP5 film; F.L. 500 mm; f/8; A 62 mm; taken with a 500 mm "mirror" lens.

M 31, THE ANDROMEDA GALAXY. Guided for 40 min on Ektachrome 400 film; F.L. 135 mm; f/2.8; A (aperture) 48 mm; lens and camera.

A FEW MINUTES AFTER FIRST CONTACT during the eclipse of Feb. 16, 1980, in India. 1/30 sec on Kodachrome 64 film; density-5 aluminized Mylar filter; F.L. 600 mm; *f*/12; A 50 mm; prime focus on 5-cm refractor.

MORE THAN HALFWAY through the first partial phase, same eclipse. 1/30 sec; Mylar filter; same equipment.

SECOND CONTACT shows the inner corona, as well as the bright chromosphere not yet eclipsed by the silhouetted moon. 1/125 sec; no filter; same equipment.

THE RED CHROMOSPHERE and several prominences at 1/1000 sec; same equipment.

THE MIDDLE CORONA, with tremendous detail in the streamers, such as the loop at about the 11:30-o'clock position. 1/30 sec; same equipment.

THE MAGNIFICENT FULL CORONA, showpiece of the Indian eclipse. 1 sec; same equipment.

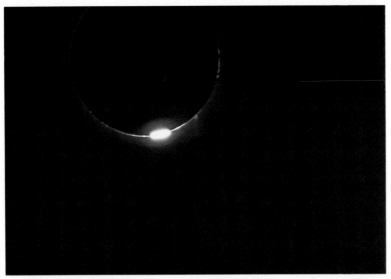

THIRD CONTACT brings beautiful diamond ring and more prominences. 1/500 sec; same equipment.

THE SECOND PARTIAL PHASE starts with the razor-thin solar crescent. 1/30 sec; Mylar filter; same equipment as the other photographs of 1980 India eclipse.

CHAPTER 4

· ·

SOLAR PHOTOGRAPHY—
The UNeclipsed Sun

The Sun, at magnitude minus-27, is 400,000 times brighter than the Full Moon and 13 billion times brighter than the brightest nighttime star. **CARELESSNESS WHILE OB-SERVING THE SUN MIGHT RESULT IN PARTIAL OR TOTAL BLINDNESS.** The Sun must *never* be viewed directly through a telescope or camera without proper filters because this would concentrate the Sun's rays on the retina of your eye, permanently damaging the delicate tissues. For this reason, you must reduce the Sun's intensity by filters or other means before viewing or photographing.

A standard measure of a filter's light-reducing power is its density. A density of 5 (not to be confused with a 5× filter, which is a very different story) reduces the light entering it by a factor of 100,000. This is about right for use in looking at the Sun.

The safest and easiest filters to use are those that are placed in front of the telescope rather than inside the instrument in the middle of the light path. Filters placed near the eyepiece are, generally, dangerous in that they are at the hottest part of the cone of light coming from the telescope's objective; they are prone to cracking in the intense heat, and that could send a devastating flash of light to your eye. In fact, there is more danger than meets the eye, so to speak. There are filters which, when looked through, seem effective because they dim our view of the solar image a lot, yet which actually transmit invisible but highly dangerous radiation whose effects turn up only later in the form of permanent eye injury.

Some telescope manufacturers sell safe filters mounted in convenient holders to fit in front of their 'scopes, and these are generally of high quality. Beware, however, of the glass filters that screw into the eyepieces of some cheap scopes, as they can be dangerous for the reasons stated above.

A popular solution is to buy quantities of aluminized Mylar, which looks a bit like thin tin foil. Some types have a density of 2.5 per sheet, meaning that two sheets must be used together, while others, with a density of 5, can be used in single sheets; all are safe for visual use. Aluminized Mylar yields a blue image of the Sun, which is something you'll have to get used to if you want to use this economical, generally high-quality material. I bought a 12-ft roll of Mylar a few years ago; several home-made filters later I'm still in no danger of running out.

Mylar should be used in front of telescopes and camera lenses, as with all solar filters; used behind eyepieces, it may melt in the intense heat as mentioned above. It can be held in place by wooden, cardboard, or metal holders fashioned to fit snugly in front of your telescope or camera lens—make doubly sure it will not slip or blow off in the wind. Try not to handle the material directly too much, as this will ruin the surface and degrade its performance, and you will have to use a new sheet. You can also hand-hold aluminized Mylar to view the Sun directly, of course.

Another popular photographic solar filter is the neutral-density filter, which is *not* for visual use. N.D. filters reduce all visible wavelengths of light by an equal amount, the amount being determined by the particular filter's density rating. As with all solar filters, a density of 5 is considered safe for photography. By nature, these filters render a natural color—much dimmer, of course, but pleasing to the eye. Not so pleasing to the eye, though, is the fact that while you are looking through the viewfinder at the Sun—focusing, composing, or whatnot—the filter is reducing *visible* radiation but letting highly dangerous *invisible* radiation pass through freely to your eye, perhaps causing permanent damage.

The solution is to hold a piece of thin Mylar or a piece of *overexposed* and *completely developed black-and-white* film in front of the camera eyepiece while focusing and composing (color film will not do). Granted, the solar image will be dim, but you will save your eyes.

After focusing, you must still be careful to resist the temptation to look through the viewfinder with a naked eye, even though the Sun will appear dimmed. Any damage will not pain your eyes at the time, but will turn up later.

The techniques used for solar photography are virtually the same as those used for lunar photography. Because the angular diameters of the Moon and the Sun are nearly identical, the image sizes of the two will be about the same size when photographed through a given system. As with the Moon, a focal length of at least several hundred millimeters is needed to capture any detail on the Sun's surface. And there *is* a good deal of detail, contrary to popular belief.

Sunspots—great cool splotches on the Sun's surface—show up as dark spots because they are cooler than surrounding regions. Many sunspots are larger than the Entire Earth, and some can even be seen, unmagnified, by the unaided eye (unaided except for a filter, of course). Sunspots will begin to show up with lenses of relatively short focal length, and detail starts to show as focal length increases. By using projection methods with a refracting or a reflecting telescope, you can zero in on separate sunspot groups.

High-resolution long-focal-length systems will show the intricate granular structure of the Sun's surface.

An interesting project is a daily record of the Sun over a period of several days. Each day the Sun's rotation carries sunspot groups around from behind the western limb, or edge, across the solar face, and out of our sight behind the eastern limb. In addition to solar rotation, you can watch developments of the larger sunspot groups, and smaller sunspots appearing and disappearing.

Another obvious and easily photographed phenomenon is *limb darkening*. When we look at the center of the solar disk we see the Sun's hot, bright depths beneath the cool outer regions. At the limb, however, we see only these dark outer layers; therefore, the limb appears darker than the center. Limb darkening will show up with equipment of only a few hundred millimeters' focal length, and sometimes less.

Because of the Sun's intense light, you can use slow, fine-grained films and still have shutter speeds fast enough to prevent trailing. Sometimes using aluminized Mylar or other filters can lead to a curious problem, however: You might end up filtering out *too much* sunlight. If you use projection systems to get details of sunspots, chances are the *f*/ratio will be so high that you will be limited to the faster emulsions—perhaps ISO 400 or so—unless, of course, you have a clock drive. Unless you are using a neutral-density filter and thus getting a true-color image of the Sun, color films will yield false Sun colors, depending on what type of filter you use.

Exposures in photography of the Sun are determined quite simply by using the formula below.

$$f^2 = s \times t \times 10^{7\text{-}D}$$

where f is the *f*/ratio of the system
     s is the sensitivity ("speed") of the film
       in ISO/ASA rating
     t is the shutter speed ("time") in seconds
     and D is the density of the solar filter.

The same formula can also be written

$$t = \frac{f^2}{s \times 10^{7\text{-}D}}$$

when it is the shutter speed you wish to find.

Example: You are using a filter of density 5, a lens of f/4, and ISO/ASA 64 film:

$$Shutter\ speed = \frac{4^2}{64 \times 10^{7.5}}$$

$$= \frac{16}{64 \times 100}$$

$$= \frac{16}{6400}$$

$$= \frac{1}{400}$$

Thus, a shutter speed of 1/500 sec would be about right. As usual, you should *bracket,* or take a few exposures longer and shorter than the calculated exposure, just to make sure of getting it right.

SUMMARY

EQUIPMENT: In general, same as for lunar photography, plus adequate filters: aluminized Mylar, exposed and developed black-and-white film, commercial telescope filters, or N.D. filters for photography

EXPOSURE: By calculation from equation

$$f^2 = s \times t \times 10^{7-D}$$

as explained in text

FILM: Fine-grain if possible, but anything will work

REMINDER: It is of the utmost importance that you realize the danger involved in viewing and photographing the Sun.

CHAPTER 5

· ·

PLANETARY PHOTOGRAPHY

Photography of the planets of our Solar System is, quite simply, very difficult. Because of small angular size, details on their surfaces are very difficult to photograph (see Appendix I). A lens with 2000 mm focal length will yield an image of Jupiter only .38 millimeter across! Even with a fine-grained film and great enlargement, this small image will show only the slightest of details. It is obvious, then, that what is needed is powerful projection magnification (described in Chapter 3), by eyepiece or other means. A useful rule of thumb in planetary photography is that you should aim for an image of at least 2 mm in diameter. For Jupiter, which has an angular diameter of 40 arc-seconds, this means a focal length of about 10,500 mm (see Appendix I for image-size formulas). This means that a 15.2-cm *f*/8 reflector, F.L. 1219 mm, would require a projection magnification of at least 8.5 power.

Hand in hand with high projection magnification goes high focal ratio, as explained in Chapter 3. This, in turn, dictates long exposures, from fractions of a second to several seconds. Because of both extended exposure times and high magnification, a clock-driven equatorial mount is a must. A slow-motion control is not really needed, although it is useful. The important thing is to make sure the telescope is tracking at the right speed to keep up with the planet during the entire exposure. Check this by first watching the image through the camera's viewfinder for a period of time at least as long as the exposure will be.

The same problems crop up here as with all super long-focal-length systems—for example, in lunar detail work, as we saw in the previous chapter. Shutter vibrations and tracking errors are very noticeable, and accurate focusing is difficult. Focusing on a dim star usually works better than focusing on the planet itself. You might find that the normal camera viewfinder does not magnify enough to get a good focus, in which case you will need an auxiliary magnifying focuser, usually one that clips onto the camera's viewfinder.

If the exposure is long enough, the "manual shutter" method—the cardboard in the hand (described in Chapter 3)—is useful in eliminating vibrations.

At least as important as long focal length in planetary photography is large aperture (not to be confused with *f*/ratio). It is not so much the "speed" as the resolving power of a large telescope that is needed. The larger the aperture, the higher the image's definition will be.

All the brighter planets have their own distinct characteristics that are good targets for the sky photographer.

Jupiter's bands are easily photographed with a 15.2-cm reflector or a 10-cm refractor. Larger instruments will show increasing detail on the surface of this, the largest planet. And there is a lot of detail. Tiny spots appear and disappear in a matter of hours; the Great Red Spot swings into view once every 8 hours; intricate flumes can be seen surrounding the major surface bands. Jupiter's four brightest moons are also good targets. All these small details require long focal length, large aperture, and accurate focusing.

Saturn's ring system is one of the most spectacular of the sky's showpieces. While detail in the rings is often difficult to capture, it usually isn't hard to see the rings themselves in a photograph of any reasonable clarity. Because the rings are tilted, relative to Earth, they appear to "open" and "close" periodically. At one time their surface may be clearly seen, but a

Table 5

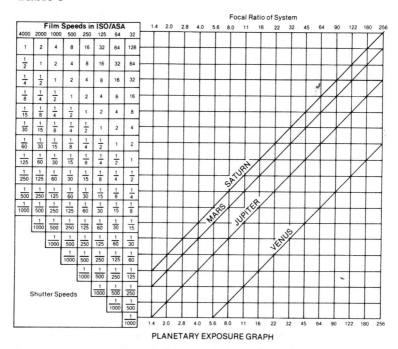

PLANETARY EXPOSURE GRAPH

few years later they might be edge-on and thus be invisible to all but the largest instruments. The divisions in the rings are best seen and photographed when they are most tilted toward us, as they will be in 1987, 2002, and every 15 years thereafter.

Detail on *Mars,* the Red Planet, is very difficult to capture on film. Because Mars's orbit around the Sun is such a long ellipse, its size as seen from Earth seems to vary from about 4 seconds to 25 seconds of arc, a change of more than six times! When the planet is at one of its close approaches to us, however, it is quite possible to get shots of the bright polar ice caps and perhaps some of the darker features.

Venus, the brightest of the planets as seen from Earth, exhibits some unique characteristics, even though surface detail is obscured by its thick atmosphere. The fact that its orbit is closer to the Sun than that of Earth allows Venus to appear in distinct phases, identical in appearance and cause to the phases of the moon. When the planet is nearly between Earth and Sun we see a thin crescent, 60 seconds of arc from one of its horns to the other. When Venus is practically behind the Sun, however, we see the planet as a near-circle only 10 seconds or 12 seconds of arc in diameter. It is interesting to photograph Venus at different stages and then compare the phases and apparent sizes; both vary a great deal.

Color filters used with black-and-white film can be of great use in planetary photography. The Great Red Spot of Jupiter, for example, is often difficult to distinguish from the surrounding surface bands. A blue filter, however, will not transmit red light, and so the spot will show up very dark in contrast to the lighter surrounding regions. Similarly, other features on the surfaces of Jupiter, Saturn, and Mars will show up better because of improved contrast when photographed through color filters. Many filters are available in mounts threaded for attaching to standard telescope eyepieces for eyepiece projection.

The choice of film for planetary photography depends on several factors.

High-contrast fine-grained film is desirable because great enlargement is often needed from the original. Such films tend to be slow, however, requiring long exposures. This in turn requires accurate driving. The greatest problem with long exposures, though, is often turbulence in Earth's atmosphere—the cause of the twinkling of stars. During a long exposure, the image of the planet wiggles and wobbles so much that it becomes noticeably blurred. All this is to say that when the seeing, or steadiness of the air, is poor, use of fine-grained slow films for extra definition can often be self-defeating.

Faster films require shorter exposure time but are often more granular, and so able to show less detail.

In other words, you will have to compromise to achieve a balance between film speed and resolution or "sharpness." Often, you may simply use medium-speed, medium-resolution film types until more advances are made in the sensitive emulsion coatings of photographic film.

The exposure graphs given in this book are fairly accurate, although, as mentioned before, it is usually wise to bracket your exposures to make sure of getting at least one or two right.

SUMMARY

EQUIPMENT: Camera with reflex focusing, locking cable release, telescope, clock-driven equatorial mount

OPTICS: Focal length long enough to yield image 2 mm in diameter or larger; aperture as large as possible—several centimeters, at least

EXPOSURE: From graph in Table 5

FILM: Should be relatively fast but must also be able to be greatly enlarged—medium-speed color-slide films are good.

CHAPTER 6

....

REACHING DEEP
INTO SPACE

It is perhaps with objects in what is known as *deep sky* that the cumulative light-gathering power of photographic film emulsions plays the most important, and often the most interesting, role. Wisps of faintly luminous gas, dim distant galaxies, clouds of interstellar dust reflecting the light of nearby stars—many of these fascinating things are invisible to the naked eye or even when viewed through a telescope, and yet it is possible to bring out detail in all of them through long-exposure photography. Indeed, it is in the areas of dim, diffuse, nebular objects such as galaxies that photography has made the largest contributions to our knowledge of the universe.

The all-around rule of thumb in deep-sky photography is that "fast" lenses are better. This doesn't necessarily mean a large aperture, as with stellar photography. What is needed here is a low *f*/ratio. Recall that this is the ratio of focal length to aperture (see Glossary). The choice of focal length usually depends on the particular subject. The famous Andromeda Galaxy, for example, which is actually twice the size of our own Milky Way Galaxy, is so large in angular diameter that its image wouldn't fit in a 35-mm-film frame if you tried to photograph it with a lens longer than about 600 mm in focal length. On the other hand, the same lens would produce an image of M 57, the Ring Nebula in the constellation Lyra, that was only a small fraction of a millimeter in diameter! Obviously, a longer focal length would be desirable here. Often, however, the need for long focal length and low f/ratio can come into conflict because a longer focal length for a given aperture means a *higher* f/ratio. You may find a compromise is necessary.

For some subjects, for example the Andromeda Galaxy, telephoto lenses available for most 35-mm S.L.R. cameras are quite suitable; often the catadioptric "mirror" lenses of about 500-mm or 1000-mm focal length are fine. With smaller objects, however, you must move up to telescope-plus-camera combinations. Usually prime-focus attachments (described in Chapter 2) are best, since projection systems (Chapter 3) would increase the focal ratio too much. The larger the aperture, the more resolving power the system will have. Homemade and commercial reflecting telescopes of apertures 15 cm and more are usually ideal for deep-sky work, especially if the f/ratio is low.

Accurate guiding is necessary because most of the time you will be using long focal lengths and long exposures. If you are shooting through a telescope, a powerful guide 'scope or an off-axis guiding system is needed, not to mention, of course, an equatorial mount with clock drive and with slow-motion control on at least the polar axis. (I have fewer deep-sky photos than any other kind. For the most part, this is due to the limits of my own equipment. To take long exposures through my homemade reflector, I would need not only a more accurate clock drive than I have but also a more powerful guiding system than the 50-mm refractor I have mounted on the main 'scope.) The setup for most photography of nebulae and galaxies is in fact similar to that for open and globular star clusters (see Chapter 2). The main difference is that for star work the emphasis is on aperture, while for extended objects (that is, non-point-sources of light, in this case galaxies and gaseous nebulae), the need is for low focal ratio.

Fast films are better than slow ones for deep-sky photography because often exposures run longer than an hour, many nebulae being very dim. Although reciprocity failure generally causes the sensitivity of fast films to drop off faster than that of slow films, in the long run the faster ones usually need less exposure time, even for extremely long exposures.

Color shots of nebulae can be spectacular. The Great Orion Nebula, for example, appears white to the eye but to color film is the bright red of glowing hydrogen clouds. The Trifid Nebula in the constellation Sagittarius shows both red and blue to the color emulsion.

Fast black-and-white films have a large place in nebular photography, too. All of them are less likely than color films to be affected by reciprocity-law failure, and many show better contrast.

SUMMARY

EQUIPMENT: Camera, locking cable release, telephoto lens or telescope, equatorial mount with clock drive, guiding system (separate telescope or off-axis)

Optics: Focal length to suit target, aperture large enough to create low f/ratio and high resolution; reflecting telescopes with camera body at prime focus are ideal, although sophisticated and not always needed

EXPOSURE: Depends on target, f/ratio, and film speed; can be anywhere from 15–20 minutes for bright nebulae to 1½–2 hours for dim galaxies.

CHAPTER 7

· ·

ECLIPSE '80—INDIA

In the humid 30-degree-C heat (85 degrees F) of the Indian coast we rolled up our shirtsleeves, glanced at our watches nervously, and made a few last-minute checks of our equipment.

A friend of mine from the American Museum–Hayden Planetarium in New York had his elaborate photographic and telescopic equipment set up right next to me. Now, he made a quick entry into his tape recorder: "Only two minutes till first contact and not a cloud in the sky. Boy, this day really turned out to be a beauty, especially after this morning's fog!"

He drew out his piece of nearly opaque No. 14 welder's glass and took a look at the Sun. The density-5 glass filter made the Sun look green, but it transmitted a surprising amount of detail. At the moment, he could see one sunspot group so large it was visible without a telescope.

I snapped one last photo of the full round Sun as the few seconds before 2:17 P.M. ticked by.

My friend switched on the tape recorder again. "It is now two-sixteen and forty-five seconds," he said, "and first contact should be any second now. There it is! A tiny flattening has occurred on the solar limb at about the five-thirty position. The eclipse of February sixteenth, nineteen-eighty, is under way."

Sure enough, plainly visible through our filter-protected telescopes was a slight, shallow indentation marring the Sun's perfect circle. I quickly pressed the shutter of my telescope-camera combination and stepped back to breathe a deep sigh of relief and anticipation.

A singular excitement accompanies first contact of a total solar eclipse when the skies are clear. All the weeks of fretting over weather data, of preparing or buying equipment, and of making travel plans and working out the logistics of an eclipse expedition finally pay off. One counts hours, minutes, seconds, watches the clouds endlessly—finally one is rewarded by actually seeing first contact.

This particular eclipse expedition had begun with a two-week tour of India. After extensive sightseeing in Delhi, Agra, Jaipur, and Bombay, we had arrived in the former Portuguese colony of Goa, 8 degrees of latitude below the Tropic of Cancer. On this morning our busses had left our hotel in Goa at 12:30 A.M. and deposited us, in a semidazed state after a 10-hour ride, in the small town of Ankola on the west coast. We had been graciously given the use of the Gokhale Centenary College, and our group of 130 dispersed over the college grounds rapidly, planting our tripods in the little squares marked off for our use in the sandy red earth.

The approach of an eclipse had been greeted with mixed responses and attitudes by the inhabitants of the subcontinent. There were scientific expeditions that welcomed the eclipse, as we did, as a rare occasion to see an important astronomical event of great beauty. Top scientists at the astronomical observatory in Hyderabad, for example, had organized an extensive program of experiments for the eclipse.

Our sightseeing trips to eighteenth-century royal astronomical observatories in Jaipur and New Delhi had underscored India's traditional interest in astronomy. These creations of the Maharajas featured 30-meter-high sundials and huge planet-finders, still highly accurate today though built entirely out of stone.

Newspapers all over the country ran articles on the eclipse for many days preceding the spectacle, informing citizens where the path of totality was to cross, issuing warnings against observing the Sun directly, and offering advice on how to view it safely. One of the more unusual suggestions appeared in *The Indian Express* of Bombay. Readers were told to "mix cow-dung in a pail of water and you will find that after it settles down it leaves a sort of semisilvered surface on the water" in which one could safely watch the Sun's reflection. We mixed up a batch of this concoction, but opted against using it for the eclipse.

Now, perched on a sandy, hot hillside we saw an Indian youth step up to my friend's telescope.

"May I look?" he inquired, stepping to the eyepiece.

"No! No!" we both cried, running to stop him. One look at the Sun's face through the telescope, equipped only with a neutral-density filter for photography, could have caused serious damage to his eyes, if not blindness. I showed him instead to my telescope, which had a visual filter on it, a piece of aluminized Mylar.

As the crescent stage progressed, I took a shot every ten minutes or so. Between times I visited other peoples' sites and equipment elsewhere on the hill, or just chatted excitedly with friends. Steadily, the bite that was the lunar limb grew larger and larger, soon reducing the Sun to a very fat crescent. A mere twenty minutes or half hour after first contact there was a noticeable change in the intensity and color of the daylight. The sky turned a rather grayer, less saturated blue, and the landscape was bathed in a thin, clear light.

By this time it was very easy to form crescent images on the ground in the shadows of our crossed fingers. Indeed, the palm thatch of the roof on a nearby hut formed hundreds of remarkable crescent images within its dappled shadow upon the sand.

We watched excitedly through our hand-held green welding glasses or the eyepieces of our Mylar-protected 'scopes as the Moon took a dead bearing on the solar crescent.

We human beings weren't the only ones exhibiting abnormal behavior, though. The huge ravens in the area became almost frenzied, flapping about and filling the air with their raucous cries.

With perhaps ten minutes to go before second contact, the

air was charged with excitement. In all directions away from the Sun the sky was a translucent green-gray, a color and light remarkably similar to that which heralds a severe thunderstorm. As if to accentuate this impression, the sea of palm trees over which we gazed was undulating in the light breeze that had sprung up, and had taken on the same electric silvery-green as the sky. One expected large, pelting raindrops at any moment, and yet there wasn't a cloud to be seen!

One minute to second contact, which was to occur at 3:38 P.M., and the solar crescent was exceedingly narrow. All filters were off now. The hair-thin crescent still blazed, but not brightly enough to hide brilliant Venus and, I noticed an instant later, Mercury.

I watched for the shadow but saw none, sensing only an approaching darkness. Then as we watched, all eyes upturned, the brilliant crescent's horns shrank and the last remaining rays of sunlight seemed to be sucked into one powerful fist of light while the inner corona sprang into view around the Moon, forming a splendid diamond ring. In a matter of seconds even this glorious white diamond was dimmed and then snuffed by the encroaching Moon. The upper edge of the Sun's chromosphere still glowed brightly as second contact, the beginning of totality, arrived, and the full corona appeared.

"Magnificent!" "Glorious!" *"Oh my God!"* came the cries from all around me. Magnificent indeed was the vibrant white corona, stretching out from the now-hidden Sun in all directions. The streamers were at least as long as the Sun was wide and showed exquisite detail in the inner and outer corona alike, much more so than at the Montana '79 eclipse. We had expected a large corona because of the high level of solar activity, and indeed it was the showpiece of the spectacle.

All this time I was clicking away at the camera furiously while simultaneously gaping through the 'scope, glancing to either side at the horizon and the sky, and whooping out of sheer delight.

It was an unusually light eclipse, perhaps because of the moisture-laden atmosphere—many observers said it was the lightest they had ever seen. There was no chromospheral light, no clearly defined shadow. One could easily have read a printed page at totality (although why anyone would want to is beyond my comprehension).

There were surprisingly few prominences. Some were visible on the upper limb at second contact and at the lower limb at third contact; but, aside from these and a few at the three-o'clock position, the profile of the Moon lacked the crimson flares and prominences we had expected and which we had seen from Montana the year before.

In what seemed like perhaps ten or fifteen seconds but was actually more than 2¾ minutes, the lower limb began to glow brightly as third contact approached. The deep red chromosphere rimmed the lower edge of the Moon for a second or two, and then a burst of light exploded around the Moon and the corona dwindled rapidly to a mere ring, the third-contact diamond ring.

Then the brilliant white gem itself broadened into a blindingly bright smile—the solar crescent—and daylight returned.

After posttotality hugging, kissing, and crying, we returned briefly to our equipment and pretended to direct attention to the growing crescent. The partial phase was a total anticlimax, however, and before long only the most stolid eclipse chasers were left alone on the sunny hill for the remaining half hour or so of the eclipse.

The considerable amount of time I had spent beforehand preparing for the eclipse expedition to India really paid off. I had lathe-turned a camera adapter to fit my 35-mm Olympus OM-1 single-lens-reflex camera body to my Tasco 5-cm refracting telescope. It was the same optical equipment I had used at the Montana eclipse, but this was a much more secure setup than the flimsy wooden contraption I had put together for Montana. I had made a wooden cell for the aluminized Mylar filter for the partial phases, stronger than the cardboard cell I used in '79, and completed it with a clean, scratch-free piece of Mylar.

Perhaps even more important, I had gone over my routine carefully. I had taken several practice shots, watching through the viewfinder to determine how much time was needed to allow the camera-telescope combination to settle down between advancing the film after one shot and making the next. I later settled upon 8 seconds as a safe interval—I was not inclined to repeat all the double images I had of the Montana eclipse. At that rate I would have time for about twenty shots during the 2 minutes 42 seconds of totality. As it turned out, I managed to squeeze in five or so extra pictures during the excitement.

Although in Montana I had gone from short exposures to long exposures only, for India I practiced going down the entire shutter-speed scale and back up it again. This way, I would be near the short exposures at the end of totality—which is what I would need for the third-contact diamond ring.

Everything in fact went very smoothly. Not a single picture was ruined by vibrations, and very accurate focus was achieved by using a special fine-grain focusing screen, made by the camera's manufacturer, in conjunction with a magnifying focuser. One problem showed up later, however—a prominent glare, introduced by the lens system, that affected all bright spots but especially the diamond rings. Those shots were almost ruined. This is just something to keep in mind next time I find myself under the Moon's shadow.

After discussing the eclipse at great length over the course of the next few days, we generally decided that by far the showpiece of the India 1980 eclipse had been the tremendous and intricate corona. We had expected something along those lines, and we had been rewarded. We were somewhat disappointed, on the other hand, with the relative absence of large prominences. All this shows is how much each eclipse differs from all others.

A great deal of the fascination and excitement eclipse chasers feel comes from not knowing exactly what to expect. There is always the dread of bad weather; yet even aside from that, no two eclipses are the same. Until the actual long-awaited minutes of totality, one can only speculate on what shape and size the corona will be, what peculiarities it will display, how many prominences there will be and how big, whether there will be a diamond ring and, if so, how long it will last—the possibilities are infinite.

Virtually all eclipse chasers can identify each eclipse they have seen. Indeed, it is a standard game at eclipse-chasers' get-togethers to see who will be the first to identify the eclipses in the slide show. "Montana '79!" or "Canberra cruise!" will be shouted out by the audience as the picture flashes on the screen. The clues, of course, are the particular shape of the corona, certain easily-recognized prominences, notable diamond rings, and so on. As any veteran eclipse viewer will tell you, there is absolutely no truth in saying about total solar eclipses that "seen one, seen 'em all."

So here's to clear skies, trouble-free equipment, and the thrill of *the hidden Sun.*

APPENDIX I

·······································

SOME BASIC TERMS

Angular size. Astronomical objects are very often measured in angular size, a term used throughout this book. Its use arises from the fact that it is often meaningless to describe a celestial object in actual, linear size. The Great Nebula in Orion, for example, is billions of times as large as our Moon, but from Earth they appear the same size—their angular diameter is the same.

The angular size of an object is defined as the angle whose sides encompass the object and whose vertex is the observer (see Figure 8). From the horizon to the zenith, or the point directly overhead, is 90 degrees. The angular distance between the "pointer" stars of the Big Dipper is about 5 degrees, while the Moon subtends an angle of about half a degree. Arc-degrees are divided into 60 minutes apiece, with each arc-minute containing 60 arc-seconds. Thus, the Moon's angular diameter could also be described as 30 minutes of arc, while the planet Jupiter's angular diameter is only 40 seconds.

You can find lists of angular size of most astronomical objects in any good star atlas.

Optics. Since lenses are essential to the astrophotographer, it would be a good idea to be familiar with the basic concepts of optics. Any convex lens (thicker in the middle than at the edges) forms an image (see Figure 9). When you burn a piece

Figure 8.   ANGULAR SIZE. (a) How two objects of different actual size (a penny and the Moon) might have the same angular size. (b) How these two objects might appear to the observer. (c) From horizon to zenith is 90°.

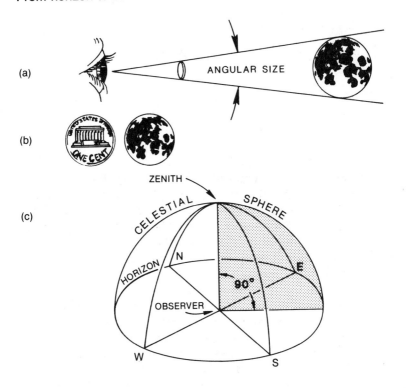

(a)

(b)

(c)

of paper by focusing the Sun's rays, the tiny, intensely bright spot of light the lens forms is actually a very detailed image of the Sun—complete with sunspots! Similarly, if you hold a magnifying glass in front of a wall directly opposite a bright window, you will see a small, upside-down (because of the lens's nature) image of the window. If you could magnify the image with a high-powered magnifying glass, you would have a refracting telescope (*refracting* because it is a lens that forms the first image by refracting, or bending, light rays).

Figure 9.   A CONVEX (POSITIVE) LENS. The image formed is one focal length from the lens.

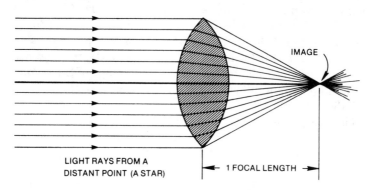

LIGHT RAYS FROM A
DISTANT POINT (A STAR)   ←— 1 FOCAL LENGTH —→

IMAGE

A lens receives many light rays from any given point, "sorts them out," and sends them to the right place on the image. The image itself, provided it is not of a single-point source like a star, actually consists of an infinite number of focused points, all of them together making up the image.

Focal length.   When you hold a lens so that the image it forms of a distant object is clearly focused on a piece of paper or a wall, the lens is *one focal length* away from the image. Focal length (F.L.) varies from lens to lens and depends on the curvature of the lens's surfaces. The great importance of a lens's focal length comes from the fact that *the size of the image depends entirely on the focal length of the lens* (and the object's size, of course!); image size is in direct proportion to focal length. This means that if you were to double the focal length of a given lens, you would also be doubling the size of the image it forms of a given object.

To determine the size of an image formed by a particular lens, use this approximate formula:

$$I = S \times F \times sin\ (1\ arc\text{-}sec)$$

where I is the image size in millimeters
    S is the angular size of the object in arc-seconds
    F is the focal length of the lens in millimeters
    and sine of 1 arc-second is 0.0000048.

This formula can also be used with values in arc-minutes or arc-degrees instead of arc-seconds. The sine values for an arc-second, -minute, and -degree are 0.0000048, 0.0002909, and 0.0174524, respectively. You must, of course, be sure to use the same one of the three units for all parts of any one calculation. Using this formula, you can determine, for instance, that a lens of F.L. 500 mm will yield an image of the Moon—which has an angular diameter of 30 minutes—of

(30) × (500) × (0.0002909) mm = about 4.4 mm.

The *exact* formula for image size is

$$I = 2 \times F \times tan\ (S/2)$$

This formula is more accurate for large angles than the first one. For example, you can use this formula to calculate the diagonal angular coverage of 35-mm film used with a lens of 50-mm focal length. The diagonal of a 35-mm film frame is 43 mm; this is our image size. From the above formula, we have

$$tan(S/2) = I/(2 \times F) = 43/(2 \times 50) = .43$$

Using a calculator or a table of trigonometric functions, we find that tan^{-1} .43, the angle whose tangent is .43, is 23.25 degrees. This is (S/2); so our angle is twice that, or *46.5 degrees*.

Focal ratio.   The *f*/ratio or focal ratio of a lens is an index of its light-gathering power for *extended* objects (nonpoint objects, such as galaxies or the Moon). It is found by dividing the focal length of the lens by its diameter (see Figure 10). The larger the aperture (the diameter of the lens) or the shorter the focal length, the *lower* the *f*/ratio and the *brighter* the image.

Suppose, for example, you had two lenses. Lens A has a diameter of 2 cm and a focal length of 6 cm, while lens B has a diameter of 2 cm but a focal length of 12 cm. The *f*/ratio of lens A is $^6/_2$=3, while that of lens B is $^{12}/_2$=6.

Both lenses collect the same amount of light from the object. Because B's focal length is double A's, however, the image formed by lens B is twice as wide (and therefore 2 × 2 = 4 times the area) as that formed by lens A. As a result, because the same amount of light is spread over a larger area,

Figure 10. A LENS'S FOCAL RATIO equals its focal length divided by its diameter.

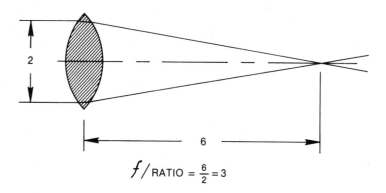

$$f/\text{RATIO} = \frac{6}{2} = 3$$

lens B's image is dimmer. Thus, the image of *any* extended object formed by lens A (*f*/ratio 3) will be brighter—four times as bright, to be exact—than the image of the same object formed by lens B (*f*/ratio 6), the higher *f*/ratio producing the dimmer image.

Coordinates in the sky. It is also useful, if you are getting involved in astrophotography, to become familiar with the motions of celestial objects. For convenience, the entire expanse of the sky as seen from Earth is imagined to be the inside of a hollow globe, with the Earth at the center. This *celestial sphere* (see Figure 11) is then marked off with coordinates very similar to the grid of latitude and longitude on the Earth. First, Earth's axis is extended into space in both directions until it intersects the celestial sphere at two points, the north and the south celestial poles. Then, Earth's equator is projected into space to form a great circle, the celestial equator, on the sphere midway between the poles.

The celestial coordinate that is equivalent to latitude on the Earth is *declination*. It measures, in degrees, the distance of an object north (+) or south (−) from the equator, with the latter being 0 degrees and the north pole + 90 degrees. Each degree is further divided into 60 minutes, with each minute containing 60 seconds. These units are equivalent to those of angular measure.

Figure 11. THE CELESTIAL SPHERE. (a) The celestial sphere, with the earth at its center, as if seen from outside. (b) Coordinates on the celestial sphere.

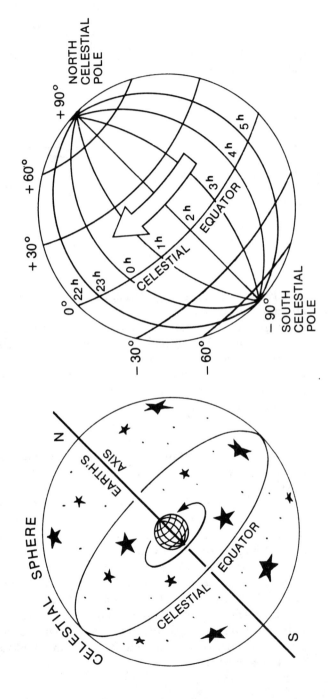

The celestial equivalent of longitude is *right ascension.* On the Earth, longitude measures the distance east or west from an arbitrarily selected line—the *prime meridian*—running north-south through the Royal Observatory in Greenwich, England. In the sky, the prime meridian is the vernal equinox—where the sun is on the first day of spring, in the constellation Pegasus. Right ascension measures along the celestial equator, in hours, minutes, and seconds, the distance of an object *east* of the vernal equinox (00 hrs, 00 mins, 00 secs); there are 24 hours to the entire sky. The minutes and seconds of right ascension are *not* the same as those of angular measure or of declination.

The right ascension and declination of most astrocamera targets—such as galaxies, nebulae, and star clusters—can be found from lists of sky objects in star atlases. These coordinates can then be used in conjunction with star charts to find the object you are looking for.

As the Earth rotates eastward, the celestial sphere, with all the stars, planets, and other celestial objects, seems to drift west at the rate of one revolution per day, always bringing objects of increasing right ascension into view until, in about twenty-four hours, everything is back where it started a day before.

APPENDIX II

· ·

GLOSSARY

Altazimuth mount. A device for holding telescopes and other optical instruments with one vertical and one horizontal axis, permitting motion only from side to side (azimuth) and up and down (altitude). (See Chap. 2, Fig. 3)

Angular size. The angle whose sides encompass an object and whose vertex is the observer's eye. (See Appendix I, Fig. 8)

Annular eclipse. Eclipse occurring when the Moon passes directly in front of the Sun for an observer on Earth, but is too far away for the umbra to touch the Earth's surface. Thus the Sun is not completely eclipsed but appears as a thin ring surrounding the Moon. (See Chap. 1, Fig. 1)

Aperture. The diameter of a lens or of a telescope's objective. Not to be confused with *f*/ratio; the two are often used interchangeably in photography. Given the *f*/ratio and the focal length of a lens, you can find its aperture by using the simple equation

$$A = \frac{F.L.}{f/ratio.}$$

Barlow lens. A negative lens used to increase the power of a given telescope eyepiece.

Bracket. To take several photographs at different exposures to ensure obtaining at least one correctly exposed picture.

Cable release. A device for tripping the camera's shutter without touching—and thus shaking—the camera. Most cable releases also have a lock to hold the shutter open for time exposures.

Celestial equator. The projection of the Earth's equator onto the celestial sphere. (See Appendix I, Fig. 11)

Celestial poles. The two intersections of the Earth's axis of rotation with the celestial sphere. (See Appendix I, Fig. 11)

Celestial sphere. The imaginary globe of celestial objects surrounding the Earth. Half of the celestial sphere is visible at any one time from any one place on Earth. (See Appendix I, Fig. 11)

Chromosphere. The relatively thin red layer of the sun surrounding the photosphere, visible at the beginning and end of totality during a total solar eclipse. (See Chap. 1, p. 21)

Converging lens. See *Positive lens.*

Clock drive. Electric motor attached to equatorial mounts to turn astronomical telescopes, cameras, and other instruments at the rate of one revolution per day. (See Chap. 2, p. 39)

Corona. The Sun's outer atmosphere, the large envelope of hot gas surrounding the photosphere and chromosphere. Usually visible only during totality of a total solar eclipse, on account of its dimness relative to the photosphere. (See Chap. 1, p. 21)

Declination. The celestial coordinate equivalent to latitude, measuring in degrees, minutes, and seconds the distance of an object north (+) or south (−) of the celestial equator, which is at 0 degrees. (See Appendix I, Fig. 11)

Density. (1) The opaqueness of an image on photographic film. Longer exposures produce greater density (see *Reciprocity*). (2) A number indicating the opaqueness of a filter. For visual use with the Sun, a density of 5 is considered safe. (See Chap. 4)

Diaphragm. The device inside a camera lens that varies its aperture and, therefore, its *f*/ratio.

Diverging lens. See *Negative lens.*

Eclipse. Event occurring when one celestial body, for example the Earth or the Moon, casts its shadow on another body.

Effective focal length (E.F.L.) The working focal length of a *system* of lenses, such as the telescope-eyepiece-camera setup used in eyepiece projection. (See Chap. 2, p. 47)

Equatorial mount. Device for holding telescopes and other astronomical equipment with one axis—the polar axis—parallel to the Earth's axis of rotation. Equatorially mounted instruments follow the apparent motion of celestial objects by swinging around their polar axis. (See Chap. 2, Fig. 4)

Extended object. Celestial nonpoint object, that is, an object with definite angular size (unlike stars).

Eyepiece projection. (1) Method of using a telescope's eyepiece to project the primary image onto film in an enlarged form. Also called *positive* projection. (See Chap. 3, Fig. 7) (2) A safe method for viewing the Sun by using a telescope's eyepiece to project the primary image onto a cardboard or paper screen. (See Chap. 1, p. 26)

Field of view. The area visible through a camera viewfinder or a telescope eyepiece.

Film speed. The sensitivity of photographic film to light. Measured in ASA or ISO ratings, which are identical. (ISO designates the International Standards Organization.)

Focal length. The distance from a positive lens or mirror to the focused image it forms of a very distant object. (See Appendix I, Fig. 9)

Focal ratio. The ratio of a lens or mirror's diameter to its focal length. Used as an indication of image brightness for extended objects—low *f*/ratios yield bright images. (See Appendix I, Fig. 10)

f/stop. A camera lens-aperture setting indicating *f*/ratio. Each *f*/stop corresponds to an exposure factor of two: A 50-mm lens at *f*/2 has twice the aperture *area* of a 50-mm *f*/2.8 lens, and thus lets in twice the amount of light.

Guide star. Star used as a reference for tracking celestial objects during time exposures. (See Chap. 2, p. 43)

Guiding. Method of making small changes in tracking speed during a clock-driven time exposure to make sure of getting a photograph without signs of trailing or blur. (See Chap. 2)

Lunar eclipse. Eclipse occurring when the Moon, revolving in its orbit around Earth, passes into Earth's shadow and is partly or totally blocked from direct sunlight.

Magnification. See *Projection magnification.*

Magnitude. A number representing the apparent brightness of a celestial body. A difference of one magnitude is a difference of about 2.5 times in total brightness. (See Chap. 2, p. 45)

Negative lens. A lens that is thinner at the middle than at the edges. Also called a diverging lens, because it tends to make incoming parallel rays diverge.

Negative (or Barlow) projection. Method of using a negative lens to project a telescope's primary image onto film in an enlarged form. (See Chap. 3, Fig. 7)

Objective. The main light-gathering, image-forming optical element of a telescope. Usually either a lens or a mirror.

Off-axis guider. Device, mounted at a telescope's eyepiece holder during prime-focus photography, which allows one to guide through the *same* telescope. (See Chap. 2, p. 47)

Partial solar eclipse. Eclipse occurring when the Moon passes in front of *part* of the Sun for observers on Earth; in fact, the Moon's penumbra touches Earth but its umbra misses completely. (See Chap. 1, p. 19)

Path of totality. The path traced along Earth's surface by the Moon's umbra during a total solar eclipse. Observers must be stationed along this path to see the sun totally eclipsed. (See Chap. 1, Fig. 1)

Penumbra. That part of the shadow of a celestial body (*e.g.* the Moon or the Earth) from which only part of the Sun is seen. (See also *Umbra*) (See Chap. 1, Fig. 1)

Photosphere. The highly luminous surface layer of the Sun, the sharp disk that one sees through a dark filter. (See Chap. 1, p. 21)

Piggyback. Method of attaching a camera to the side of an equatorially mounted, clock-driven telescope to track celestial objects during time-exposures. Guiding is done through the telescope. (See Chap. 2, p. 43)

Polar axis. See *Equatorial mount.*

Pole. See *Celestial poles.*

Positive lens. A lens thicker at the middle than at the edges. Also called a converging lens because it tends to focus incoming parallel rays, forming images of objects. (See Appendix I, Fig. 9)

Primary image. The first image formed by a telescope's objective. Not necessarily the final image, which might be projected, etc.

Prime focus. Method of sky photography in which a camera body is used to hold the film at the primary image of a telescope's objective. (See Chap. 2, Fig. 5)

Projection.   See *Eyepiece projection* and *Negative projection.*

Projection magnification. The amount of enlargement of the primary image in afocal, eyepiece, or negative projection. (See Chap. 3)

Prominences.   Huge incandescent eruptions in the photosphere of the Sun. Visible only with special filters or during a total solar eclipse. (See Chap. 1)

Reciprocity, Law of. The characteristic of ideal photographic film which states that the density of an image is in direct proportion to its exposure time. (See Chap. 2, p. 39)

Reciprocity failure. When film is used for very long exposures, its sensitivity decreases during the course of the exposure, so that the Law of Reciprocity no longer holds. Color balance may also be affected. (See Chap. 2, p. 50)

Reflecting telescope. A telescope whose objective element is a concave mirror, usually parabolic.

Reflex focusing. Feature found on most high-quality cameras allowing the image to be viewed on a ground-glass screen before the exposure is made, thus permitting accurate focusing and composing.

Refracting telescope. A telescope whose objective element is a positive lens or series of lenses.

Resolution. A measure of or judging a given film or optical instrument's ability to render fine detail.

Right ascension. The celestial coordinate equivalent to terrestrial longitude, measuring in hours, minutes, and seconds the distance of an object east of an arbitrary zero reference, the Vernal Equinox. (See Appendix I, Figure 11)

Shutter speed. A camera setting indicating the length of time the shutter stays open to expose the film. For example, a setting of 1/125 sec is twice as long an exposure as 1/250 sec.

S.L.R. or Single-lens reflex. Type of camera in which a mirror sends light rays from the picture-taking lens to a ground glass for accurate focusing and composing. The mirror flips out of the way during the exposure, allowing the light to form an image on the film.

Terminator. The line separating the Moon's sunlit day-side from its shaded night-side.

Total solar eclipse. Eclipse occurring when the Moon passes in front of the Sun for observers on the Earth, blocking it out completely; that is, the moon's umbra touches the Earth. (See Chap. 1, Figs. 1 and 2)

Trailing. Image blur due to subject motion caused by Earth's rotation.

Umbra. The part of a celestial body's shadow (such as the Moon's or the Earth's) from which no part of the Sun is seen. (See also *Penumbra.*) (See Chap. 1, Fig. 1)

APPENDIX III

. . . .

A WORD ON FILMS

Film technology is advancing so rapidly now that any comprehensive list of films for astrophotography, with their special characteristics, would be rapidly outdated. As this edition goes to press, for example, two new ISO 1000 color films, which hold great promise for astrophotographers, have recently appeared on the market (see *Sky and Telescope,* December 1983). This story will repeat itself again and again. For this reason, I chose not to recommend specific films in the text, but rather to keep suggestions qualitative, such as "slow and fine-grained" or "as fast as possible."

You will want to experiment with different films anyway. Some very useful black-and-white films are high-contrast copy films, technical pan, and graphic-arts materials.

For the purposes of this book, "slow" film refers to ISO/ASA ratings of, say, 25 to 50; "medium" or "moderate speed" covers ISO 64 to, say, 150; and "fast" or "high-speed" designates ISO 200–400 and more.

Astronomical journals such as *Sky and Telescope* and *Astronomy* provide the best means of keeping abreast of recent advances in light-sensitive materials, as do photography magazines.

APPENDIX IV

SOME OTHER READING

All about Telescopes by Sam Brown. Barrington, N.J.: Edmund Scientific Co., 1976. An excellent, information-packed introduction to astronomy, telescopes, and telescope optics, with many diagrams.

Astronomy magazine. Milwaukee Astromedia Corp. Aimed at amateur astronomers and the informed layman. Full of nice photographs.

Astrophotography, by Barry Gordon. Richmond: Willman-Bell, projected for publication in 1985. Thorough coverage by a long-time teacher of the subject.

Cambridge Encyclopedia of Astronomy, ed. by Simon Mitton. New York: Crown Publishers, Inc., 1978. A comprehensive reference volume that is also very readable by those with little technical background.

Eclipse, by Bryan Brewer. Seattle: Earth View, Inc., 1978. Written especially for the February 26, 1979, total solar eclipse, but serves as useful guide to eclipse viewing and history.

Norton's Star Atlas, by Norton and Inglis. Cambridge: Sky Publishing Corp., 1973 (16th edition). Full of star charts, tables, and reference articles. A classic that no astronomer should be without.

Observer's Handbook of the Royal Astronomical Society of Canada, Toronto, Ontario. Published annually, the Handbook contains invaluable information on occultations, times of sun- and moon-rise and set, eclipses, etc.

Outer Space Photography by Dr. Henry E. Paul. New York: Amphoto, 1977 (4th ed.).

Sky and Telescope magazine. Cambridge: Sky Publishing Corp. You will profit immeasurably just by flipping through the *ads* in this magazine, let alone reading the various and diverse articles.

JAMES LOWENTHAL was twelve years old when he made his first telescopes out of cardboard tubes and magnifying glasses, training them on neighboring apartment buildings in New York City. While a freshman at Stuyvesant High School, he ground the mirror for a 6-inch Newtonian reflecting telescope, with which he still scans the Connecticut skies. He has chased eclipses in Montana and India, spending more than four minutes in the shadow of the Moon. Currently a sophomore at Yale University, he is majoring in astronomy and physics.